Reaching for the Light

GW00660190

Reaching
for the
Light

A Guide for Ritual Abuse
Survivors and Their Therapists

Emilie P. Rose

The Pilgrim Press
Cleveland, Ohio

The Pilgrim Press, Cleveland, Ohio 44115

© 1996 by Emilie P. Rose

The publisher gratefully acknowledges permission to reprint excerpts from the following copyrighted material:

From *Diagnostic and Statistical Manual of Mental Disorders Fourth Edition*. Washington, D.C.: American Psychiatric Association, 1994.

From "Ritual Abuse: What Is It?" by Healing Hearts. Copyright © 1992. Bay Area Women Against Rape, 357 MacArthur Blvd., Oakland, CA 94610.

From "Ritual Abuse: A More Accurate Language and Its Implications" by Elizabeth Power. Copyright © 1993 Elizabeth Power. Reprinted with permission of E. Power and Associates, MPD/DD Resource and Education Center, Nashville, TN.

"Davida Angelica Roared," copyright © 1991 by Beth A. Richardson. Used with permission of the author.

From Ntozake Shange, reprinted with the permission of Simon & Schuster, Inc., from *for colored girls who have considered suicide/ when the rainbow is enuf* by Ntozake Shange. Copyright © 1975, 1976, 1977 by Ntozake Shange.

From "Reprogramming Worksheet" by Caryn StarDancer from *Survivorship*, vol. 3, no. 8 (August 1991). Copyright © 1990 Caryn StarDancer. Used with permission of the author.

From "Sitting with the Shattered Soul" from *Pilgrimage: Journal of Personal Exploration and Psychotherapy* 15:6 (1989). Used with permission of the author.

Library of Congress Cataloging-in-Publication Data

Rose, Emilie P.
    Reaching for the light : a guide for ritual abuse survivors and their therapists / Emilie P. Rose.
        p. cm.
    Includes bibliographical references and index.
    ISBN 0-8298-1079-x (alk. paper)
    1. Ritual abuse victims—Rehabilitation. 2. Ritual abuse victims—Rehabilitation—
    Case studies. I. Title
RC569.5.R59R67 1996
616.85'82—dc20
                                                  95-52521
                                                     CIP

for
Ginger, Beth, and all my helpers
and for all the kids

Contents

Foreword

We have all seen the stories on television or on newsstands. Adults and children claim to have been brutally abused in their homes, neighborhoods, day care centers, even churches, by robed, chanting, bloodthirsty cults who perform bizarre rituals in the name of Satan. The rituals are said to include the torture, rape, and murder of innocent victims. We hear whispers of human sacrifice and cannibalism, too shocking to believe but too compelling to ignore.

In our culture it's sometimes hard to separate reality from fantasy. We do know worshipers of Satan exist. But do these people actually form cults and abuse children in rituals?

The answer is yes. Cult ritual abuse is a terrifying reality whose existence few of us want to believe. The idea of sadistic pedophiles, lust murderers, and worshipers of Satan gathering together to engage in group sexual perversion and homicide with children is unthinkable. Our sane minds cannot comprehend such unspeakable acts, and we demand answers: "Where are the bodies?" "Where are the witnesses?" "How could such heinous crimes involving so many people escape detection?" Our very souls cry out in primitive horror, "How could anyone do this to children? It cannot be true!"

But it is true. Not every account is true, and not every instance is accurately or honestly reported. However, we front-line professionals who work with victims of crime, trauma, and abuse hear these stories. Some of us back away out of skepticism, denial, or a driving need to preserve our own innocent worldview. This does not stop the children and the adults from coming forward with their stories. Those of us who have listened to their grim tales have examined the reports in closer detail. We have learned that cult ritual abuse does occur. Children suffer, and God is defiled.

All the professionals I know have had the same gut-wrenching aversion to believing reports of cult ritual abuse. We have hoped desperately, just as you are hoping, that this is just some urban legend, an incredible myth. Someone would surely have reported the incident. Someone would certainly have been arrested. Clearly there must be some other explanation for what we have heard and seen.

We have looked hard for alternative answers, and still do. Most of us carefully examine our methods of creating close, trusting relationships in therapy. We watch for trance states, too-eager compliance, subtle suggestions being mutually reinforced, secondary-gain issues, and false accusations. I know I have encountered some of this, but not nearly enough to dismiss all the accounts of abuse. As we have struggled with our own biases, conducted research, sought consultation, and practiced with rigor and caution, we have also learned more about cult ritual abuse.

Too many cases remain that have been corroborated in some compelling fashion, even after our caseloads have been critically analyzed. Locally and nationally, we have seen sets of siblings make the same reports to different therapists; photographs of satanic marks and scars on children's bodies; photographs of torture instruments and ritual sites; identical descriptions of rituals from the same cult, given by children and adults who did not know each other; and too many more chilling instances that prove cult ritual abuse is a real and dangerous phenomenon.

We have learned that witnesses *have* come forward, that people have told. We have written the child protection reports, and cult survivors have risked their lives going to the police. The reports have been ignored, and witnesses have been labeled crazy or pawns of unscrupulous therapists. Just as the Nazis dismissed eyewitness accounts of the Holocaust as "atrocity propaganda," those in the United States with a vested interest in denial have labeled cult survivors, and those who listen to them, as hysterical witch hunters.

We have learned how the various types of cults form, function, and remain undetected. We have discovered that these people find one another the same way all underground networks recruit and connect, whether for drugs, robbery, or sexual perversions. We have learned how the crimes are concealed; the "fieldstripping" of bodies by shredding them into smaller and smaller parts has become gruesomely familiar. We have observed that planting false memories and disinformation applies much more to sexual offenders than it does to therapists, and that cult leaders use mind control, drugs, and hypnosis to distort memory and reality. And we have all been astonished by the ease with which one can get away with things done in secret, especially if those things are bizarre.

The methods the cults use to silence children are devastatingly simple and more masterfully sadistic than any fictional horror Stephen King could devise. Just cutting the tongue out of a cute animal can delight cult members and forever silence a child. Rituals in which "bombs" are implanted in a child's body—which will blow up if the child tells about the abuse—are cruelly effective. Telling this child she will know if the bomb is about to explode, because she will feel very scared and nervous, turns the threat into an incredibly powerful self-fulfilling prophecy. The child thinks about telling, remembers the "bomb," and becomes scared and nervous.

We professionals certainly have not relied only on our observations about cult ritual abuse. We have learned facts as well. Cult ritual abuse is not a myth, it is a crime, and several states have created laws against it. Illinois passed Public Act #87-1167, which defines, cites exclusions, and specifies penalties for the crime of ritually abusing a child. Such laws were drafted after legislators learned of prosecuted cases of cult ritual abuse, from resources like Michael Newton's *Raising Hell: An Encyclopedia of Devil Worship and Satanic Crime*, which documents instances of satanic crime in the United States and abroad.

We have also learned that the facts are not always what they seem. The McMartin day care case, in Los Angeles, was unsuccessfully prosecuted, and is regarded in the media and popular culture as a case study in false accusation. When forensic anthropologists were able to examine the site of the alleged abuse after the trial, however, they found physical evidence of the tunnels to the ritual site, just as children had described them. A cauldron was also found, again just as reported, but it was quickly dismissed as merely a "large pot." The media were and still are silent about these discoveries in particular, and about cult ritual abuse in general.

The saddest fact of all is that there is no way to account for far too many missing children. In 1984 the U.S. Department of Health and Human Resources estimated that 1.8 million children disappear every year. Ninety-five percent of these are classified as runaways, and 90 percent of them return home within two weeks, leaving 171,000 children per year growing up on the streets. Five percent of the remaining children are classified as abductees. Seventy-two thousand of these are victims of parental kidnappings that result from bitter custody disputes—though this is hardly a reassurance of these children's safety.

What of the rest of the missing children? Where are the other eight thousand abducted every year who are never seen again? Within all these categories of missing children, there is certainly room to believe at least a few hundred or even a few thousand children die at the hands of ritual abusers. We know that serial killers and sadistic pedophiles exist. Some of these people have affiliative needs, and these needs are met in cult rituals. Abductees or throwaway children no one cares about satisfy their violent cravings to torture and kill.

Margaret Smith, the author of *Ritual Abuse: What It Is, Why It Happens, How to Help*, conducted a survey of fifty-two adult survivors of cult ritual abuse. Four of the respondents mentioned another form of abuse they were forced to engage in: luring children from playgrounds for kidnapping. For those of us who have worked with cult ritual abuse, reports of abductions of children, transients, and other vulnerable adults are fairly common. Missing-children posters are becoming an all too familiar part of our landscape. Where are these children? Where are their bodies?

Certainly, cult ritual crime is a relative rarity. It alone cannot account for the plethora of abductions, child rapes, and mutilation deaths. It is, however, related to the growing social problem of random, brutal violence and murder. Remember that for every cult ritual survivor who seeks help, there are many more who act out their horror on other victims. Cults create serial killers, rapists, and child abusers, some of whom continue with cult activity and some of whom strike out on their own. As cult ritual abuse continues unabated, the number of cult-injured predators increases from generation to generation. I believe that in years to come our society will pay a great price for its denial, in the form of more abductions, bizarre abuse, and grotesque murders.

We must avoid panic or a rush to judgment on cult issues. But we must also have the courage to stare evil in the face. This book will help us do that. It is gentle and strong, and it tells the truth about recovery without trying to frighten. The author writes with compassionate discretion about the spiritual degradation and enormous physical suffering that are the reality of cult ritual abuse. The book will undoubtedly be attacked. And it will undoubtedly save lives. I wish all who read it the spiritual gift of discernment as they learn more about the painful reality that is ritual abuse.

Renée Fredrickson, Ph.D., L.P.

Preface

In the fall of 1989 I entered a tunnel of darkness, terror, and pain that changed my life, history, perceptions, values. It was a journey that, at times, I thought I would not survive.

I had everything I needed in life—a loving relationship, a good job, a graduate degree, a place to live, friends, and a church family. But something was wrong—I was afraid to be in crowds of people, unable to make phone calls to people I didn't know, having disturbing dreams, afraid for anyone to touch me. I didn't know that I was in the midst of major depression and that years of denial, dissociation, and repression were getting ready to crumble.

I began having intrusive flashbacks that illuminated a childhood of horror. This flashback-childhood was inconceivable next to the "perfect childhood" I thought I had known. The flashbacks stripped me of everything—my history, my trust, my spirituality, my personhood, my God. It called into question the decisions and life choices I had made. I was in crisis and wondering whether I could continue to live.

I came to know that the "perfect childhood from the perfect family" had been like what is known in the theater as a *scrim*—a piece of fabric used as a backdrop, which creates the illusion of a solid wall or scene; when lit from behind, the scrim becomes transparent and reveals another scene. I had only been able to see the surface, the beautiful scenes of a "perfect childhood," until my brain began releasing fragments of what had really happened. Behind my scrim of perfect pictures was a scene of destruction, pain, and ritual abuse.

I was faced with the task of reframing my life and my identity. I came to see that, like the scrim, my life had been one-dimensional. There were missing pieces, both information and depth of personality. So much of me had been "frozen" in the abuse that after the "thaw" I felt like a different person, more alive, aware, able to make sense of things that never made sense before. And I met parts of me I had not known before. I experienced a new depth, a new range of feelings, and a new multidimensionality.

On January 1, 1992, in the midst of that healing, I began writing this book. One of the things that had given meaning to the pain of the recovery from abuse was the possibility that someday, if I made it through, I might be able to help others to heal. That promise helped me through some very hard times. Writing the book was, in a sense, an affirmation of the hope and healing I found in my journey, adding meaning to the suffering I had endured.

As I have continued to heal from the ritual abuse, I have come to like who I am, to appreciate who I have become, more than ever in my life. The book is a witness to the truth that no matter what we have experienced, we can heal from it. We can really have a life. We can become whole people living and loving and sharing our lives with others.

This book was created out of the wisdom of survivors, therapists, and other helpers who have been learning together how to recover lives devastated by ritual abuse. Persons working in the field of ritual abuse recovery are pioneers forging paths in the wilderness. Survivors, therapists, and other helpers are both teachers and learners in this process.

I am deeply grateful to the many helpers who have been a part of my healing journey, who have been my teachers and colearners. Without you, I might not have survived the process of healing. To the healers and teachers, the therapists and spiritual friends, the friends and family members, I say thank you. You each helped to "love me into being."

I am grateful to everyone who contributed to the process of writing this book: to Marie Fortune, Martha Whitmore Hickman, Ann

Thompson Cook, Emily B., Mary Catherine, and Wendy, who read versions of the manuscript and made invaluable suggestions; and to the many survivors who shared with me their stories, their courage, their wisdom, and their encouragement. Special thanks go to those who wrote for this book—Mary, Wendy, Anna, Adam, Tracy, Michelle, Claire, and Sister Hope.

My gratitude goes to the members of the task force on ritual abuse who supported this endeavor and who helped me remember the reasons for finishing the book.

And to my family of choice—thank you for your unconditional love and support through the long days and nights of healing.

Introduction

To the Survivor

If you are a survivor picking up this book, you are probably experiencing a mixture of feelings—fear, confusion, shock, apprehension, numbness, anger, curiosity, denial, or sadness. You may be a ritual abuse survivor whose therapist has asked you to read this book. You may have just picked it up off the shelf in a bookstore.

You may be someone who thought you were all alone. Or at least "really sick" or "crazy." You are not alone. Whoever you are, your feelings are valid, and it is okay to feel them. I honor whatever you are feeling. I am one of you.

Know that whatever you are feeling or remembering, you are not crazy, you are safe today, you are not alone; hope and light await you at the end of the journey.

This book is not meant to be *the answer* to all your needs. As ritual abuse survivors, our needs are very great. In addition to this book and other written resources, we can utilize help from friends, professional helpers, support groups, and other survivors. But, as ritual abuse survivors, we also can affirm that no matter how wounded we are, we have within us everything that we need to heal. We have within us the same strength, creativity, desire to live, resourcefulness, imagination, and orneriness that kept us alive when we were children. Those attributes are within us now, helping us to survive. They will help us transform our lives of woundedness and pain into lives of healing and love.

To Therapists, Helpers, and Other Supporters

Though ritual abuse is very old, its treatment is a new field. Until recently, resources for the treatment of ritual abuse survivors have been nonexistent. Survivors and therapists have been teachers and learners together, learning to cope with and heal from the effects of ritual abuse.

This book contains the collective learning and wisdom of many survivors, their professional helpers, their friends and families. Although much of the book is written directly to survivors of ritual abuse, it is intended also to be a tool for therapists, counselors, pastors, and other supporters of survivors. The book provides basic education about the nature of ritual abuse and its effects on people who have experienced it. The chapters focus on several of the issues that are unique to survivors of ritual abuse. It is important to survivors that their therapists and other helpers learn all they can about ritual abuse, its effects, and the needs for healing (and that the survivor is not functioning as the only teacher.)

If you are a therapist with clients who are survivors of ritual abuse, it may be helpful to suggest that the survivors read the book under your care, using some therapy time to work through issues which emerge during their reading.

Chapter 11, "For Therapists and Helpers," will suggest some specific things you can do to help survivors in their healing. In addition, you may want to personally work through chapters 2 and 7, "What Is Ritual Abuse?" and "Facing Evil," respectively. Ritual abuse is traumatic for helpers as well as survivors. You may find that you need time in your own therapy or supervision setting to work out your own feelings about ritual abuse. Take the time you need to care for yourself. That is one of the greatest gifts you can give to your ritual abuse clients.

Using This Book

It is my intention for this book to be used as a complement to other resources and tools for healing which you already have or will develop. Since the stages of healing are similar for different kinds of abuse, I have not attempted to duplicate the excellent descriptions of the healing process covered extensively in other resources such as *The Courage to Heal*.[1] Use these other resources as a companion to this book. I hope that you will draw from the wealth of wisdom that has begun to emerge during the last several years. (See the resources listed at the end of this book, under the heading "Healing from Abuse.")

Reaching for the Light focuses on areas of healing that are especially important for ritual abuse survivors. Each chapter contains exercises for self-reflection which will help you to develop a skill, examine your beliefs, and create safety for your healing journey. Rather than recounting stories of abuse, this book focuses on stories of healing by survivors of ritual abuse. Even so, it is often difficult to read about ritual abuse without becoming uncomfortable or being triggered.

To help create the safety you will need while reading this book, please begin with chapter 1, "The Basics." Reading it first will provide a foundation upon which you can anchor and build your healing journey.

Chapter 2, "What Is Ritual Abuse?," examines ritual abuse in light of current knowledge and the climate of denial in society.

The next four chapters present coping tools that we, as ritual abuse survivors, especially need. Because we are often isolated, without support, chapter 3, "Building Networks," discusses how we can develop our basis of support. It covers such areas as making friends, identifying and keeping boundaries, and discerning when disclosures are safe.

Chapter 4, "Kid Management," helps readers understand and develop skills for dealing with the challenges of dissociation. It tells about the survival skills that are developed in order to cope with the abuse and makes suggestions for dealing with "inner children."

Programming and mind control are often part of the ritual abuse experience. Chapter 5, "Reprogramming: Overcoming Mind Control," examines the effects of programming and how to overcome it.

Losses for ritual abuse survivors are often severe. Chapter 6, "Loss and Grief," helps the survivor assess his or her losses and begin to grieve for them.

"Facing Evil" (chapter 7), "Reclaiming Ritual" (chapter 8), and "Healing Our Spiritual Selves" (chapter 9) look at the theological and spiritual problems produced by the reality of ritual abuse. These are some of the most difficult areas of healing for survivors, and also the areas in which resources are most difficult to find. These chapters may be especially difficult to read because they touch on such deeply wounded places within us. It is all right to take your time with them and go at your own pace. It is also all right if you don't want to deal with them at all.

Chapter 10, "Long-Term Healing," identifies some of the issues that survivors face over the long healing journey. This chapter may be seen as a starting place for the next phases of healing from ritual abuse.

Interspersed throughout the book you will find stories of recovery written by courageous survivors of ritual abuse. I asked each contributor to talk, not about their abuse, but about their journeys of healing, of moving through and beyond the pain.

Finally, chapter 11, "For Therapists and Helpers," makes specific suggestions to professionals about the ways to help ritual abuse survivors.

So join me on this journey to healing. We—survivors, friends, and healers—are pioneers together. To get better, all we have to do is stay alive.

Davida Angelica Roared

Once there was a lioness whose name was Davida Angelica. Everybody called her Angel. Angel didn't roar very often. In fact, she had only roared once in her life.

It was when she was just a little cub. She was playing in the grass with her brothers and sisters, and a hunter's arrow pierced her shoulder. Angel roared in surprise, and her mother chased the hunter away.

Angel's mother tried to pull the arrow out, but the shaft broke off and the arrow point stayed in Angel's shoulder. It hurt when she walked, but in time the wound healed at the surface and Angel forgot all about what happened. Everyone else forgot too.

The only reminder Angel had of the wounding was the pain in her shoulder. But after a while, she hardly noticed it. And when she did feel the pain, she thought that all lions felt that way.

Angel grew up to be one of the favorite lions in the forest. She was gentle and kind. By the time she was a young lioness on her first hunt, she had forgotten all about the wounding. But even when she made her first kill, she did not roar like the other lions.

One day, as Angel was hunting food for her own cubs, she noticed a pain in her shoulder. She thought to herself, "What is that feeling? Have I felt it before?"

Soon the pain began to grow. Angel's shoulder hurt when she jumped out of trees or carried her cubs or ran fast to catch a deer. After several months, Angel's shoulder hurt all the time. She

Source: Beth A. Richardson: "Davida Angelica Roared," *Alive Now* 21, no. 3 (1991): 44–46. Copyright © 1991 by Beth A. Richardson. Used by permission of the author.

began to limp and her hunting suffered because she could not run fast enough. finally, she could not move at all.

The wise ones came from far and near to gather around her. They brought food for her cubs, healing herbs, and stories of the great hunters. They surrounded her with warmth and breathed strong breaths with her. Their growls swirled around her and under her, and wrapped her like a mantle of fire.

That night as the moon rose, Angel herself began to growl. At first it was a low growl, and when she raised her head, the pain stabbed through her. Then she growled a low roar. And a bigger roar. And then the growls of the wise ones lifted her to her feet and she began to *roar*.

Davida Angelica roared and roared and roared. All the lowly animals shivered in their beds. Davida Angelica roared and roared and roared, and the fur on her shoulder began to split. Davida Angelica roared and roared and roared, and the skin under the fur popped open and yellow liquid poured out of her shoulder. The liquid gathered in a pool on the ground, and in the middle of the pool was an arrow point. Davida Angelica roared and roared and roared and roared. And then she was quiet.

The wise ones looked at the arrow point, growled, and nodded, for now they remembered and understood. And then the oldest one said, "Davida Angelica, from this day forward, you will be called Davida. You have lived through a wounding. You have survived great pain with great courage. You will be called Davida the Courageous. Davida with the Roar That Heals."

Then the wise ones roared. And Davida roared with them. And they all roared long into the night.

CHAPTER ONE

The Basics

All will be well.

—Julian of Norwich, *Showings*

The purpose of this chapter is to build a common basis for reading the rest of the book. Ritual abuse is very destructive emotionally, psychologically, physically, and spiritually. When we begin to remember our abuse, we are often overwhelmed and in crisis. It is very important for us to learn to gauge the pace of our healing journey and to moderate our exposure to information about ritual abuse. At first, even the smallest trigger can send us reeling for hours or days. But as we progress in our healing, we learn to avoid unnecessary triggers and manage crises so that our lives return to a healthier, more comfortable rhythm.

It may be disappointing to learn that the speed of our healing is not proportional to the pace of our remembering. We cannot speed up the process by doing more reading, going to extra therapy sessions, having more memories. Healing takes its own time. And the parts of us inside that are growing toward wholeness and healing can help us pace our work at a manageable and comfortable level.

This chapter will make suggestions for safe use of this resource in your process of healing.

Safety and Support

The very fact that you are recognizing that you are/might be a ritual abuse survivor means that you have some amount of safety and support in your life. Without a sense of safety and feelings of support, you would still be protected by the defenses that have protected you until now: denial, dissociation, amnesic barriers, addictions, and all the other coping mechanisms you created to survive your abuse.

The fact that you are reading this resource indicates that you are ready for healing. But foremost in this process of healing from ritual abuse are the cornerstones of safety and support. No matter how much safety and support we already have, we can always use more. And in order to do our work in healing, it is important to continue to build these areas of our lives.

SAFETY

The need for safety can be summed up in the questions, "Do I feel safe about my life today? Is my home safe? Do I feel safe with myself? with my friends? If I am still in touch with my family, do I feel safe with them?" If you are experiencing fears, they may stem from present circumstances or they may be feelings from a long time ago. It is important to examine and evaluate these fears to find out their source.

Ask yourself what you are afraid of: "Is there something in my life today that is not safe and that needs attention? Am I feeling unsafe because I need a new lock on the door?" If there is something concrete that you can do to address the fear, take the action to make your life safe today. If you cannot pin the fear to anything specific, it may be feelings from a long time ago that are seeping into your awareness today.

A therapist can help you determine what your fears are about and how to deal with them. If you do not have a therapist you trust, it is important to find one and develop a safe relationship with him or her before embarking on the journey into your past. (See "Finding a Good Therapist" on page 166.)

SUPPORT

Support—feeling that we are not alone, that others know and believe and care about us—is the key in feeling safe today. Because we were deeply wounded, support is a difficult but necessary area for us to develop. Building a network of support means trusting others enough to develop relationships with supportive people. These people can be there for us if we need help, someone to talk with, someone to be with.

For many of us, a therapist is the first person in our support network. We may add to that support network other survivors and close friends to whom we disclose our abuse. We need to know that when we are feeling sad, angry, lonely, overwhelmed, or desperate, someone will be there. The more people we can add to our network, the safer we will feel. (A support network is like the safety net stretched out beneath the high-wire act at the circus.)

If you feel as though you are "working without a net," make a list of the people you consider to be a part of your support network. Then make a second list of people you might like to have in your support network. Think through strategies to add some people from the second list to your list of supportive people. Make a goal to approach two people per month (or make your own goal) to investigate their willingness to support you.

As you develop your network, you may need to educate your supporters about what you need and do not need. Be specific in asking for what you need. Some survivors need people to talk to, people who call regularly and ask how things are going, people to play with, people available to nurture through safe touch or a listening ear. Also be clear about things you do not need. For example: "I don't need you to fix me. I just need you to listen." Or "I will tell you when and what I need. You do not need to guess. You don't have to take care of me. I can take care of myself." (You will find other ideas about building a support system in chapter 3, "Building Networks.")

Safety in Reading This Book

Do not plunge into reading this book until you feel, both internally and externally, enough support and safety to face difficult feelings or memories associated with your abuse. It is necessary and essential to be grounded enough to work on deeper levels than you may have worked before.

Set boundaries for yourself that honor your safety. Here are some examples of ground rules and boundaries for using this resource:

1. Ask my therapist to help me know when I am ready.
2. Read the book in my adult self. No kids allowed. (This book is not appropriate material for the inner child to read.)
3. Decide on time limits for reading—thirty minutes, one or two hours at a time.
4. Decide on a safety plan if something I read upsets me or reminds me of something that happened in my abuse. (If I get triggered, I will call my therapist, a support person, etc.)

Write your own guidelines in your journal or inside the cover of this book.

WARNING SIGNS

When you see this warning sign, $\underline{\bigtriangledown}$, it means that the material that follows may include things that can trigger flashbacks, memories, or programming. Be sure that you are in your adult and that any younger parts of you are safe. Call a support person if you need to, and evaluate whether you are safe to read that part now.

Since we ritual abuse survivors can be easily triggered, know that I may not have marked every one of your triggers with a warning sign. Plan ahead of time for what you will do if you are triggered. Write your safety plan inside one of the covers of the book so that you can refer to it easily.

Imagination and Healing

This resource includes exercises and suggestions for using imagination to help you heal from your abuse. Some of these ideas may challenge the part of you that is very logical. You may already be wondering how imagination can be a part of healing. Current experiential treatment methods, workshops for survivors, and numerous resources on working with the inner child[1] are showing us the powerful uses of creativity and imagination for healing old wounds. (Chapter 4 will elaborate on the use of imagination and healing.)

Most of us adult survivors were able to use creativity and imagination as a way of coping with and surviving our childhood trauma. Those same powers of the mind can work in our healing today.

However, when highly logical persons use these methods, they often make the assumption that what is happening is not real—that they are making it up, creating the effect by thinking, or the like. If you are one of these highly logical (or skeptical) people, use your logic to observe that many people successfully use creative, imaginative techniques. Give yourself permission to suspend judgment for now, to let go and try out your creativity, to trust that you are allowing inner healing to occur (even if it feels unfamiliar and uncomfortable at first).

The Inner Child/Children

Many of you are already familiar with the concept of the inner child and use it in your process of healing. As ritual abuse survivors, some of us may discover that we have inner *children*. There are many ways to look at and interpret this recognition as a tool of healing.

Many survivors of ritual abuse are clinically diagnosed as having dissociative identity disorder (formerly called "multiple personality disorder"). (Not all ritual abuse survivors cope with their abuse in this way. The reactions to trauma are as diverse as there are survivors.) These diagnoses reflect coping skills that the survivor developed to survive the abuse. Many of us who are diagnosed with dissociative disorders prefer to describe the multiplicity as the inner children who helped us live through our abuse and who live within us now.

One way to think about this is that we were not able to process the trauma that was happening to us while it was occurring. Our brains protected us, enabled us to survive, by creating amnesic barriers around the parts of the brain where that experience was "stored." These amnesic barriers encased "pockets" of trauma which were kept in our unconscious mind until we were ready to deal with the trauma. We can imagine each trauma pocket as an inner child who is at the age and level of development that we were when we experienced that particular incident of abuse. Thus, we may find that we have inner children to care for as we recover from our abuse. These inner children are brave survivors who helped us get through our abuse. We will look more closely at the effects of trauma and working with inner children in chapter 4.

The Healing Process

Ritual abuse survivors go through the same stages of healing that are necessary for other abuse survivors. For ritual abuse survivors, healing may take longer (five to ten years, as opposed to three to five years for "regular" abuse). The thing to remember is that ritual abuse survivors *do* heal. We do get better. We can move through and out of the emergency stage[2] and begin to reclaim our lives. We can *have a life* (some of us for the first time) and enjoy it. We can live gracefully in freedom.

Our healing process includes hurt, terror, anger, and sometimes overwhelming pain. We survived our abuse. And we can have courage that we will be able to survive the healing. With some physical wounds (deep cuts, broken bones, torn muscles), the healing process involves a time of pain. This is true, also, for the deep psychological, emotional, and spiritual wounds of abuse. Pain is part of the healing process. It will not kill us. We can survive the pain of healing.

RITUAL ABUSE FLASHBACKS

Flashbacks are part of posttraumatic stress disorder. Flashbacks and memories of trauma are frightening whether you are an incest survivor, the victim of a car accident, or a war veteran. But ritual abuse flashbacks are even more terrifying and traumatic. Because the memories of ritual abuse are so intense, bizarre, scary, and sometimes unbelievable, the experience of remembering the abuse is traumatic in itself.

For persons who are moving from "regular abuse" memories to ritual abuse memories, some adjustments need to be made to keep yourself safe. Ritual abuse flashbacks are terrifying, intense, and possibly dangerous. Set up safety procedures with your therapist or helper. For example, try not to have flashbacks or go into memories when you are by yourself. Call someone on the phone if you feel as though you are going into a flashback. Learn to reschedule memories for times when you are with your therapist or support person (see "Rescheduling Memories" below). Make a list of your safety procedures and share them with your support people.

RESCHEDULING MEMORIES

The ability to postpone and reschedule flashbacks is a helpful skill to develop. After time, you may be able to sense when you are getting ready to go into a flashback. Some survivors are able to tell when a memory is coming by particular physical signs (tingling limbs, dizziness, yawning, facial twitching, rapid breath, etc.) or emotional signals (terror, overwhelming anxiety, extreme anger, etc.). Over time you will be able to recognize these signs.

If you are not in a safe place to have a memory, try the following steps to reschedule the flashback:

1. Acknowledge the feelings and thoughts that you are having. Say to yourself, "I recognize that there is information needing to come out. But right now it is not safe to remember or to receive this information."

2. Thank the parts of you that are wanting to give you the information and tell them that right now is not a good time to do it. "Thank you for coming forward to tell me this information. I am glad you felt safe enough to want to tell me. But right now, I am . . . [at work, not in a safe place, at a movie, etc.]."

3. Set a time to hear the memory. "I can't receive the information right now, but I want to make another time to listen. I will listen . . . [at my therapist's office tomorrow at 10 A.M., tonight at 7 o'clock when I am safe at home, etc.]." Be specific about the time and the place.

4. Keep the appointment. Honor your commitment to be there at the time and place that you arranged.

In the case of a sudden trigger, you may not be able to use this technique. In that case, if you are able, try to remember that the abuse is not happening today and that you are safe. Call a support person to talk about what is happening.

Wendy's Flashbacks

Flashbacks are one of the worst parts of being a ritual abuse survivor. They are debilitating, terrifying, and horrible. My flashbacks have changed over the past several years. For the first year I had *lots* of memories, and it took weeks to recover from some of them. I didn't know what to do when I had a flashback, so I'd get scared and hide. I still hide in a corner in my bedroom if I have a really bad memory. But usually I try to get a friend on the phone. It is very helpful to talk to someone from my present when I'm engulfed in some horrible scene from the past. That person can remind me I am not four years old and I am safe in the present. These days, memories are few and far between, and when I have one it doesn't knock me out for as long as it used to. After years of flashbacks, I know I'll survive them and they can't hurt me, no matter how real they seem.

Feelings of Despair and Hopelessness

Most of us have times when we feel despair and hopelessness. These feelings are normal, given the abuse we went through. Know that you are not alone in your feelings.

 Any very intense feelings such as despair, pain, hopelessness, or wanting to hurt yourself may be a feelings flashback. It may be that you are experiencing old feelings—ones that you could not feel as a child or youth when the abuse was happening. If you are having a feelings flashback or if you are feeling overwhelmed, ground yourself in today by calling someone, going outside and feeling the ground beneath your feet, looking at a special picture or note from someone you care about. Wrap yourself in a warm blanket and put on soothing music.

The feelings will change as you let yourself go through them and get to the other side. You will not feel this way forever. It is worthwhile to feel the pain or whatever you are feeling because healing is on the other side. Feelings of peace will be yours again.

AN EMERGENCY PLAN

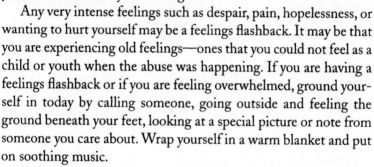 For some of us, the memories are so painful or full of negative messages that we may become suicidal. It is very important for you to live. It is not okay to hurt yourself. *All of us, together, gain strength from our collective survival of this terrible abuse.* To give up now would be to let the abusers win. We have lost too many and too much for us to lose you now.

Make a plan for times when you feel suicidal. It might include any or all of following strategies:

1. Make a list (with phone numbers) of people to call.
2. Take the steps you need to make your environment safe. For example, safety-proof your house. Get rid of anything with which you think you could hurt yourself. If you are not safe doing this alone, ask a housemate to help. Or ask a friend to come over to help you.
3. Make a no-harm contract with your therapist or helper. Here is an example of one such contract:

No-Harm Contract

I contract with [name of therapist or other helper] not to hurt or kill myself or anyone, inside or outside, intentionally or not intentionally. If I feel as though I may hurt myself, I will not do so until I have talked to [name] in person. This contract is binding for all parts, known and unknown. [Specify dates and any other terms of the contract.]

[Sign and date the contract with your therapist or helper.]

4. Make a list of things to do when you feel desperate or suicidal. Include activities that comfort and nurture you. Here is an example of one person's list:

What to Do When I Feel Desperate

- Feel.
- Breathe.
- Don't hurt myself. Call my therapist.
    Phone number: _____.
- Call the local crisis line. Phone number: _____.
- Call _____. (List names and phone numbers.)
- Hold my bear.
- Go to a safe place.
- Pray.

- Color.
- Listen to soothing music.
- Go outside.

5. Make a list (when you are feeling good) of reasons you want to live.

Keep copies of your lists and your no-harm contract with you so that you can read them when you are feeling overwhelmed.

If you are feeling suicidal, hang on for now. The feelings will change. It is okay to have them; it is not okay to act on them. You are valuable to many people in the world, and your life adds something to all of our lives. Life on the other side of the pain is worth going through it. If you cannot trust this statement, let others of us trust it for you: Life is a gift, and your life is valuable.

UNDERNEATH THE SUICIDAL FEELINGS

 As you grow in your recovery, you may be able to step back and notice whether there are patterns to your feelings of suicide and despair.

It is *very important* to take these feelings seriously, to treat yourself gently, to tell someone what you are feeling and thinking, to refrain from hurting yourself or anyone else.

If you are certain that you are not in immediate danger, you and your therapist or helper may be able to look more closely at the signs and signals. The feelings may be a signal that part of you is trying to get your attention. As we look underneath our suicidal thoughts and feelings, many of us find memories trying to surface or painful feelings needing to be released. For some survivors, there is a direct correlation between the suicidal fantasies and the memory of abuse that follows.

Recognizing the links, the messages, and the patterns hidden within your feelings of self-harm and despair can increase your sense of power and defuse the hopelessness that accompanies the low times. Learn to decode the signals your feelings are giving you. Learn to read yourself. If your suicidal feelings are connected to a memory, find help and let the memory come. You will feel much better after the memory is out.

Remember: It is okay to have the feelings. Feelings surface because they need to be felt. It is not okay (ever) to act on feelings of self harm. To do so would harm not only you, but also everyone around you who cares about you. It is important for you to live. You can survive the feelings. You are not alone.

Boundaries with Family of Origin

If you were ritually abused by your family of origin, it is very important to evaluate your relationship with your family and set appropriate boundaries. If you still have regular contact with family members, you may want to consider an initial no-contact boundary until you are sure that you are safe to be in contact with them. Contact with abusers frequently results in feelings of confusion, denial, and fear. Also, contact with cult perpetrators may trigger destructive programming, a form of mind control that was introduced as a part of your abuse. (See chapter 5 for more information on programming.)

If you do not know the identity of your abusers, it may still be advisable to be careful about contact with your family, at least until you are able to assess your level of internal and external safety.

If your family does not know about you having remembered abuse, it is usually best for you not to tell them, initially, about your memories. Take the time to evaluate with your therapist whether disclosures and/or contact with your family are safe for you and your recovery. One therapist has advised, "Don't tell any member of your family unless you are ready for all of your family to know."

These suggestions may seem harsh and extreme. They are, however, the best thinking of people who have worked with ritual abuse survivors over time. They are meant to be suggestions for internal and external safety for the healing journey.

So we end this chapter where we began—with safety. As you continue your journey in healing, remember that your safety is more important than the speed with which you heal. Healing has its own timetable. And every day you live is another day toward healing your wounds. May these words be a part of your healing.

CHAPTER TWO

What Is Ritual Abuse?

They are *afraid* of children; that the children might know something they don't want to remember, namely that they have done something without thinking.

—Elie Wiesel

You do not have to look very far to find experts who "don't believe in" ritual abuse, especially satanic cult abuse. The recovery, speaking out, and belief by society of those who have been ritually abused is a fairly recent phenomenon. Ten or fifteen years ago, a person making such claims was labeled crazy (i.e.: schizophrenic, psychotic, hysterical, delusional, etc.). These people were often "treated" with a heavy drug regimen, shock treatment, and/or institutionalization. The purpose of the treatment was to rid the patient of the symptoms (which we now know were memories and consequences of abuse).

The development of the study of posttraumatic stress disorder (PTSD) after the Vietnam War laid the foundations for another look at clinical models of treatment and the discovery that some of these "crazy" people might be telling the truth. Instead of being psychotic or delusional, such people might have PTSD and its effects—flashbacks, body and auditory memories, high anxiety, startle response, etc. (See appendix A for the definition of posttraumatic stress disorder.)

But along with the onset of the treatment of trauma survivors—including war veterans, incest and sexual abuse survivors, and ritual abuse survivors—came a premise that had to be accepted: People do horrible things to each other, to animals, and to children.

"Polite" society does not talk about, much less want to believe, that such things as rape and murder occur within the families and among the acquaintances of "normal" people. Thus, a society based on the denial that people can commit horrible, degrading acts has to overcome this denial in order to acknowledge the presence of and assist the victims of these acts.

At the time of this writing, it is commonly accepted that war veterans suffer from posttraumatic stress disorder. It is becoming more widely acknowledged that incest occurs far more frequently than once was suspected. (Current estimates are that one in three females and one in four to seven males experiences sexual abuse during childhood.) And ritual abuse is just beginning to be uncovered and spoken about.

What Is Ritual Abuse?

Because the awareness and treatment of ritual abuse survivors are so new, there has yet to be agreement among survivors and professional people on a common definition of ritual abuse.

Healing Hearts defines ritual abuse as

> any systematic pattern or practice by an individual or a group toward children (or adults who are emotionally and/or physically unable to resist or escape) that constitutes abuse of power in order to harm and control the victim. Such practices may sometimes appeal to some higher authority or power in justification of the actions taken. This abuse may be mental, physical, emotional, spiritual, or sexual.[1]

(See appendix A for a more complete definition of ritual abuse by Healing Hearts.)

David W. Lloyd, J.D., has developed this working definition of ritualistic victimization:

> The intentional, repeated, and stylized psychological abuse of a child accompanied by criminal acts directed against the child,

typified by physical assault and sexual victimization of the child,
cruelty to animals, or threats of harm to the child, other persons,
and animals.[2]

Types of Ritual Abuse

The term *ritual abuse* is commonly used to characterize satanic, Ku
Klux Klan, or other cult activity where the abuse happens in and
around a ritual setting. But ritualized abuse can occur in a variety
of ways. Elizabeth Power points out that there are several categories of ritual abuse: (1) familial, (2) fraternal, (3) theological, and (4)
political.[3]

In familial ritual abuse, there is repeated abuse by one or more
members of the family. For instance, if a child is raped every Sunday morning before going to church, she learns that when Sunday
morning comes, she is in danger. This abuse is ritualized in that it
follows a pattern of repeated behavior. The child is conditioned to
the ritual of the abuser's behavior and abuse. Since the abuse happens prior to a religious activity, there may be significant spiritual
wounding of the child. (This in itself is a type of ritual abuse.)

Fraternal ritual abuse is primarily perpetrated by organized
groups characterized by secrecy, organized rules, and points of initiation. The functioning of the groups is usually highly ritualized.
(For instance, certain vows or covenants and ceremonies are part of
the environment of the group.) Power points out, "Any secret society where advancement equals increasing power and requires increasing secrecy is vulnerable to perpetrating fraternal ritual abuse
of some sort."[4] Fraternal groups that have been known for ritualized abuse include some Masonic groups and the Ku Klux Klan.

Theological ritual abuse is based on a particular theological point
of view. Power notes that theological ritual abuse "encompasses
repeated injurious acts committed by a member of a specific theology against another person." Satanic ritual abuse obviously fits into
this category. Also, Christian groups such as those led by Jim Jones
or David Koresh perpetrate theological ritual abuse. In addition,
this category can include theologically based groups that use abu-

sive means to enforce behavior. These groups use "ritual abuse such as chronic shaming to control membership [in a group]. Such shaming, when applied from childhood on, has the same dissociative effect as the more often thought of rituals employed by those labeled satanists."[5] Thus a conservative Christian church can perpetrate ritual abuse by attempting to control children with its doctrine and its biblical interpretation. (For example, the use of the verse "Spare the rod and spoil the child" to justify regular beatings.)

Political ritual abuse is carried out by persons with a particular political viewpoint or political process. It includes groups such as criminal societies (including various segments of organized crime), governments (including various segments of the intelligence and military communities), and terrorist groups. Former hostages of political groups tell of torture, deprivation, and programming that are similar to the experiences of children abused by satanic groups.

RITUAL ABUSE IN THIS RESOURCE

Although this resource will focus primarily on ritual abuse by theological groups such as satanists, it may be helpful to note that the effects on the survivor of any ritual abuse are often the same. Posttraumatic stress disorder, dissociation, shame, spiritual conflicts, isolation, etc. are the results of severe trauma, no matter what the source of that trauma.

As you read this book, remember that ritual abuse survivors of various categories have more in common than we have differences. Feel free to adapt the language to fit your experience. Focus on the effects of the trauma and the invitation to heal rather than on the specifics of the abuse.

SATANIC RITUAL ABUSE

Since much of this resource is written from the perspective of those who have experienced satanic ritual abuse, we will look briefly at it here.

If we open our eyes and ears to those in the survivor community who are speaking out about their abuse, we learn that satanism is much more common than society would like to believe. Resources are beginning to spring up to tell the stories of ritual abuse survivors, but we are in the beginning stages of knowledge.

Several definitions of satanism can be found in written sources. The *Encyclopaedia Britannica* defines it as "worship of Satan, or the devil, the personality or principle regarded by the Judeo-Christian tradition as embodying absolute evil in complete antithesis to God."[6] Psychiatrists Walter Young, Roberta Sachs, Bennett Braun, and Ruth Watkins write that satanic cults are "intrafamilial, transgenerational groups that engage in explicit satanic worship which includes the following criminal practices: ritual torture, sacrificial murder, deviant sexual activity, and ceremonial cannibalism."[7]

If we unpack the definitions above, we can better see the elements that make up satanic ritual abuse.

Intrafamilial, transgenerational groups. Satanic abuse often occurs within an extended family system. Multigenerational groups that use traditional forms of satanism pass this tradition down through many generations. People who have been abused by these traditionalists may have been born into the cult family and subjected to the abuse for their entire childhood.

Other survivors may have been exposed to a traditional satanic cult for several years but not throughout their entire childhood. These survivors may have been brought into the abuse by family or family friends who participated in the cults for a limited period of time.

Another type of satanic activity is perpetrated by those who are "dabbling" in satanism. These dabblers include teenagers and adults who may or may not be connected to the formal rituals or belief systems of traditional satanism.

Criminal practices. The worship of Satan per se is not a criminal act. Religious freedom is protected by law. What is illegal is any *criminal practice* that is connected with the worship of Satan (or any other religion). These criminal acts by satanists typically include physical and sexual abuse, torture, kidnapping, mind control, murder, and cannibalism.

Explicit satanic worship. Worship that follows traditional satanism includes ritualistic acts that are abusive to the victims. Victims may be animals or people of any age or gender. Ritualistic acts include enactments of (primarily) Christian observances in which satanic theology and beliefs replace the Christian theology and beliefs. Satanic theology is Christian theology used in destructive ways.

Sexual and physical abuse are incorporated into rituals. The Christian communion ritual is reenacted using human flesh and blood. Where positive qualities and values are preached in Christian forums, values such as hate, death, and evil are valued in satanic circles.

Signs and Symptoms

You do not have to have actual flashbacks to indicate that you have been abused. Bennett Braun has developed an indicator called the "BASK model." [8] BASK stands for behavior, affect (feelings), sensation, and knowledge. Braun suggests that dissociation (a result of trauma) creates a process by which events such as trauma are experienced through parallel but not necessarily integrated ways of knowing. This means that knowledge (picture memory) is not the only way of knowing about abuse. A survivor may have feelings of terror with no picture memory of the abuse or a body memory without an emotional response. There may be knowledge of the event with no feeling attached. Or one's behavior alone may indicate that trauma has occurred. There are many ways of knowing;

survivors do not have to have specific memories to know that ritual abuse has happened.

Other indicators that abuse may have occurred include:

Sexual problems or woundedness.
Sexual addiction or sexual anorexia.[9]
Eating disorders.
Aversion or attraction to matters concerning death or the occult.
High levels of dissociation.
Losing time or signs of dissociative identity disorder (formerly multiple personality disorder).
Abuse by several members of the family and/or people outside the family.
Extreme symptoms of posttraumatic stress disorder.
Fear of the dark, especially at sundown or at the time of the full moon.
Increased agitation, despair, or crises at times that concur with the satanic calendar.
History of mental illness or addiction within the family system.
Chronic depression or suicidal ideation.
Fear of doctors, police, ministers/priests, morticians.
Nightmares, sleep disorders.

Many of these signs and symptoms are also present in those who have been sexually abused or who have experienced other forms of trauma. This list is not meant to prove that you were ritually abused. It can, however, provide helpful validation if there is a part of you that is trying to tell you about the abuse.

Traumatic Memory

It is normal to have difficulty with evidence that you have been ritually abused. Disbelief and denial are parts of the healing process, just as they were among the creative forces that helped you live through the abuse.

Remembering those long-ago events may seem like a dream. Trauma is difficult for human brains to process. When trauma happens to a child, the memory is dealt with in a different way than in an adult brain, because children's brains are not yet fully developed. The developmental stage of the child also affects the way the trauma is stored.

For example, trauma in children younger than thirty-six months is not remembered in words. Researcher Lenore Terr found that "the type of traumatic event bore a significant influence upon whether and how completely a child would be able, verbally, to remember what had happened."[10] Terr found that trauma that occurred in short, single events were able to be remembered verbally. But abuses that happened over a long period of time or that were repeated events reduced both the ability to remember and the accuracy of the memory.

Terr found, however, that among preschool children with documented trauma, "behavioral memory (fears, play, reenactment, dreams) is almost universal. No matter what the age of the child when he [or she] experienced a terrible event . . . , the child repeatedly behaved in a fashion consonant with that event."[11] For adults, this behavior memory can be seen in the signs and symptoms listed above.

For many of us, these behavioral memories may be our only "proof" that something happened to us. There is often little external validation of our abuse. Some of us may have verification such as scars or marks on our body, the confession of an abuser, or a sibling who has similar memories. More frequently we must work through the remembering and healing processes without such validation.

This uncertainty and lack of knowing (in a literal sense) are among the most difficult aspects of dealing with ritual abuse. We must walk a narrow path between, on one side, believing in ourselves so that we can heal and, on the other, knowing that we do not have absolute proof and verification.

We have to learn to trust and believe our inner wisdom, our inner knowing. If you were ritually abused, a part of your healing is believing that the abuse happened. It helps to have therapists, friends, and support people who believe you. But ultimately it is not for anyone but you to determine whether you were ritually abused. Finally, you must believe yourself.

Denial and Backlash: "People Say It's Not True"

Controversy is raging over memories of abuse that were repressed and subsequently retrieved. It is common to see talk shows or read magazine articles that debate whether certain memories are true or false. There are statements by "experts" that ritual abuse does not happen. These discussions often upset, unsettle, and confuse survivors of abuse.

In the argument over true and false, survivors lose. We may spend so much time analyzing and agonizing about whether a particular memory happened just the way we remembered it that we cannot process the feelings that came with it. We may need to acknowledge that memories may not be exactly true, but that what happened is generally true. Terr writes, "In my view, a visual misperception, a chronological mistake, or a mistaken motivation does not make a memory false."[12]

Research has demonstrated that traumatized children may recount incorrect details about what happened to them. But the heart of the truth, the fact that something happened, cannot be disputed. "False memory does not come complete with the findings of psychological trauma—returning perceptions, behavioral reenactment, trauma-specific fears, and futurelessness."[13]

In the midst of the controversy surrounding abuse, we can remember that *we* are the experts. We are the experts because we are the ones who went through the abuse and survived it. We are the ones who bear the psychological signs of trauma. We are the ones who must know and trust the truth within us.

Society in Denial

Society is steeped in the denial of abuse. When we look at history, we see that society routinely resists the truth through denial and backlash. The truth about sexual abuse has been alternately discovered and denied by the psychiatric community about every thirty-five of the last one hundred years.[14] Sigmund Freud was among the first in the modern psychiatric community to "discover" in his patients a pattern of father-daughter incest. After his initial findings were reported, he was publicly challenged by colleagues who did not believe that such things happened. He later recanted his findings, rationalizing that he must have been wrong because "it was hardly credible that perverted acts against children were so general."[15]

Roland C. Summit regards ritual abuse as the ultimate challenge to credibility. He writes, "One development in recent history has become a last straw for professionals otherwise prepared to accept 'ordinary' sexual abuse."[16] During the past twenty years, people have finally begun to believe the testimony of sexual abuse survivors. But as reports of satanic ritual abuse have emerged, denial has increased. The atrocities of satanic ritual abuse are so *unbelievable*. They push the very edges of our capacity to believe, to comprehend. And so ritual abuse is the last straw in "this abuse stuff." People cannot believe satanic ritual abuse, so they won't believe any of it.

Societal denial is at work concerning the Holocaust. During World War II the Allies had information that the Holocaust was occurring. But not until the end of the war and the discovery of the concentration camps did the reality of what had happened sink in. And now, fifty years later, there is still discussion about whether the Holocaust happened at all. A poll by the American Jewish

Committee found that "one-third of Americans are open to the possibility that the Holocaust did not happen."[17] And that is even in the presence of the existing evidence—the pictures, the survivors' personal accounts, the death camps, the bodies, and the Nazis' own detailed recordkeeping.

Holocaust researcher Deborah Lipstadt said, "If the history of something like the Holocaust is vulnerable, any history is vulnerable."[18] If people do not believe that the Holocaust happened, it is not surprising that people do not believe that ritual abuse occurs.

But ritual abuse is true. We know that fact intimately. And we who have survived the torture and the beatings and the horrible truth of our abuse can and must survive the resistance against our truth. Someone asked Elie Wiesel, a Holocaust survivor, why he keeps telling the story of the death camps. He said that he keeps telling the story not to change the world but to keep the world from changing him. We tell our stories to keep the world from changing what we know to be true: that ritual abuse happens and happened to us. That we choose the way of healing and truth today.

Our healing today is one item of proof that ritual abuse exists. If ritual abuse were not true, then we would be patients working through a therapist's deceit in an imaginary process of healing. We would be getting emotionally, psychically, and spiritually worse, not better. But we are getting better. If ritual abuse were not true, we would be increasingly sick (delusional, neurotic, disturbed) rather than increasingly healthy. Our healing and ever-greater wholeness are witness to the freedom that we gain from knowing the *truth* about what happened to us.

"But My Abusers Seem So Normal"

What about the people who perpetrate ritual abuse on others? "My abusers seem so normal." They probably are normal—on one level.

Most of us grew up in families that looked "normal," that were respectable, sensible, upstanding, moral members of the community. It is extremely difficult to comprehend how such people could be participants in ritual abuse. In fact, it is nearly impossible to comprehend without thinking that such abuse must have been passed down from one generation to the next as an extreme, horrible form of dysfunction or illness.

If our abusers were members of our family, our extended family, or our family's circle of friends, we may feel that there are two of each person—the normal one and the perpetrator; the daytime one and the one at night; the good, loving person and the bad, abusive person.

It is possible that just as you were able to split off from the abuse and create an amnesic barrier around it, abusers "forget" the abuse they have perpetrated. One can deduce that if your parents were abused as children, they would have developed the same coping skills you did in order to survive. (This "forgetting" does not in any way take away an adult's responsibility to protect a child rather than abusing her or him!) Thus the abuse could be passed down over generations, each generation creating the next generation's dual life.

(Until you. For some reason, you are remembering. The cycle of violence stops with you and your recovery.)

You may feel devastated, homicidal, frightened, sad, or even compassionate about the people who hurt you. These feelings are all normal. It is natural for you to feel any or all of these feelings. This is an important part of your healing.

You may also spend a lot of time trying to understand how they could have done that to you. Or trying to understand who they *really* are. Or trying to figure out why they did it, whether they remember, or what they think of you.

You may never be able to find the answers. Ritual abuse just is. It does happen, and it is inexcusable, incomprehensible, and senseless. It does not make sense because it cannot make sense. It just is.

It Really Does Happen

I believe—and increasing numbers of those in the helping professions, law enforcement agencies, and general population believe—that ritual abuse *does* happen. There are too many of us coming forward with the same stories of torture, sacrifice, sexual and physical abuse, and details of rites for ritual abuse to be a fabrication. There are too many cases of children today who are telling the stories of having been ritually abused in their child care facility or their church nursery.

Historians and anthropologists speak of the same types of activities happening in other cultures and earlier in human history. There is no reason to believe that our culture should be exempt because of its sophistication or modernity. We do *not* live in a "kinder, gentler world." People still make war on other people; kidnap, torture, and dismember others; and use sexuality to gain power over and degrade children, youth, and adults.

Ritual abuse *really does happen*. May our speaking out and healing from our abuse help stop it from happening to others.

Trust and Breathe

Becoming aware of any kind of cruelty and abuse, especially ritual abuse, may leave you in a state of shock. There may be days that you can think of nothing else. There may be times when you feel confused, disoriented, and numb. Or you may feel hopeless and full of despair.

Be gentle with yourself. Believing and accepting that ritual abuse happened to you is, perhaps, the most important step toward your healing. Once you believe and accept, you can move on to the other stages of healing, and eventually to having a life of your own.

If you can do nothing else in this time of struggle, try to remember to trust and breathe. Trust that it will be okay. Trust your therapist (or whomever you can trust). Trust yourself and the healing machine that you are. Trust that you will get through this, that you can live through the healing. Trust those who have gone before you on this journey to wholeness. If you find you cannot trust, let us trust for you. Hang on and live and feel and heal just for today.

And breathe. Breathe in the air that sustains you. Breathe deeply and let go of fear and hopelessness. Breathe in trust and strength. As long as you are breathing, you are alive. Breathe in life and promise of life.

All you have to do today is trust and breathe. Trust . . . and breathe.

CHAPTER THREE

Building Networks

You made us to be / companions, / sharers of bread, / to gather /
and to break / and to be astonished / by the flavor breaking forth.
—Jan L. Richardson, *Shared Journeys*

Our abuse kept us isolated and prevented us from learning how to take care of ourselves and our lives. One important part of healing is developing healthy support systems. We no longer have to do it alone. In fact, our healing will be easier and faster if we create networks of support and use them as we need them.

Building networks of support is a challenge of recovery. The skills we learn as we create our networks are skills that we will use the rest of our lives.

Relationships

Our abuse taught us that relationships are situations in which we are betrayed, hurt, dominated, humiliated. We may have never had healthy relationships. Often our adult relationships include abuse, inequality, codependency, and reenactment of our abuse.

Healthy relationships include trust, mutuality, honesty, and vulnerability. They are dependent on the commitment of each participant to work toward health in his or her own life. In our healing from ritual abuse, we need relationships with people who will be our friends, who are trustworthy, who will believe us and listen to us. We may find such people in our support groups, in treatment, in twelve-step programs, in our faith community.

Frequently, one of the first healthy relationships we have is with our therapist or primary helper. When the relationship with the therapist is a healthy one, we have an opportunity to learn skills of relating. Within this context, the therapist can model a healthy relationship. We observe honest communication and healthy boundaries; we learn how to trust another human being.

Remember that it is okay to trust today. We have within us the ability to discern whether someone is safe for us to invite into our lives. If we listen to the truth within us, we can learn to hear and trust the voice that says, "This person is safe. It is okay to talk with him," or "This person is creepy. I need to stay away from her."

As we learn to trust others and expand our pool of relationships, we are able to begin to identify persons that we would like to include in our support network. Some of these people are folks who have experienced woundings themselves and are farther along the path to healing. Others may have a deep well of spirituality and can offer us steadiness and support. Still others are rich with compassion and the ability to hear our pain.

We can build our networks of friends and support people by doing things together—talking, sharing mutual experiences, playing, going out for a cup of tea or a sandwich. As friendships build, our network of support expands.

LEARNING TO BE FRIENDS

Some of us have never had a chance to experience the development and richness of a friendship. The scars of our abuse left us with fears of intimacy on the one hand and lack of boundaries on the other. As we grow in our recovery, we discover that we have difficulty finding the middle ground between distance from and fusion with others.

Becoming friends with another person can give us support, nurture, fun, community. And along the way, it can be a learning experience. Being friends is a skill that we have to learn, like tying our shoes or playing an instrument. Since we did not learn how to make friends in childhood or adolescence, we must learn it as adults. As we find people we want to be friends with and begin to get to know them, we discover the areas we have to work on in our skills.

Healthy friendships usually involve such qualities as honesty, trust, loyalty, compassion, supportiveness, and humor. They also involve such skills as verbal communication, problem solving, maintaining healthy boundaries, conflict resolution, having fun, and healthy confrontation.

Persons lacking friendship skills will eventually run into a difficulty that needs to be resolved within the friendship. But even normal, healthy people have difficulties from time to time; that is the nature of human relating. Every friendship sometimes has problems that need to be worked out.

The process of working through misunderstandings and difficulties, though painful at times, is what teaches us the skills we need to be friends. Going through the process also brings friends closer together as they work through difficult times to attain resolution. The bumps and bruises of longtime friendships reveal the places of strength in those relationships.

Anna's New Friends

When I was little, I did not learn much about friendships. I had friends, but my family moved a lot and I rarely continued my friendships after we moved.

Later on, my friendships were colored with my relationship addiction. I inevitably either became addicted to a friend or I let the friendship fade away because I did not have any interest in it.

After getting sober from my addiction and entering my

recovery from my ritual abuse, I found that making friends was really hard. I had never experienced long-term, functional relationships with people. Any misunderstanding usually ended the friendship, because I had never learned to work through a conflict with another. It was easier to drop the whole relationship than face the pain of disagreement.

When I went to codependency treatment, I was introduced to the concept and skills of healthy confrontation. (They called it a "carefront" because you don't confront someone unless you care about the relationship.) It was hard, but I began to learn to give and receive confrontation and to work through conflict in relationships.

I have brought this learning back to my relationships in the real world. I am still not very good at working through crises with friends. But I no longer throw away friendships just because there is conflict. And because of that, I am experiencing friendship and intimacy that I never had before.

CONSTRUCTING RELATIONSHIPS

1. Think about the relationships you have that you consider to be valuable. What is it about the relationship that makes it valuable to you?
2. Are there people with whom you would like to be closer? How can you further nurture that relationship? (If you feel safe, talk to that person about your ideas.)
3. Make a list of the positive qualities you bring to a relationship.
4. Make a list of the relationship skills you have.
5. What are the qualities and skills that you would like to develop further in yourself? List them.
6. Pick two or three skills and/or qualities you would like to target and talk with your therapist, helper, or trusted friend about how you can work on these.

Boundaries

Boundaries are invisible walls around us. Although they are a part of our safety, they are not for the purpose of keeping people out or us in. They are changeable and permeable, depending on the people we are with and situations we are in. Boundaries are an important part of healthy relationships, helping us to define who we are and who others are in relationship to us. As we develop our support networks, we need boundaries to ensure that our relationships are mutual, healthy, and appropriate.

Normal children develop boundaries as they grow from infancy and begin to differentiate themselves from their parents and the objects around them. Abuse survivors have never had a chance to develop healthy boundaries because their individual space was continually violated by persons with power. Healing from abuse includes a process of learning to identify and develop healthy boundaries in our lives.

There are several types of boundaries to identify. The principal ones are physical, emotional, and internal boundaries.

Physical boundaries tell us and others the physical proximity with which we are comfortable and safe. They may vary from person to person, depending on the relationship and the emotional closeness with the other person. To become aware of your physical boundaries, note the point you become uncomfortable when someone approaches you. Is it two feet away? three feet? one foot? Observe the distance apart that you feel most relaxed when talking to a friend, an employer, a stranger.

Emotional boundaries help us know what is safe and appropriate to share with another person. These also vary from one person to another. Boundariless persons may tell everything to everyone. As we develop emotional boundaries, we are able to choose what is appropriate to talk about with whom. Think about the kinds of things you share with your therapist or primary helper. Would you disclose all of those things to someone you recently met? Which of these things would you discuss with a coworker? with your best friend?

Internal boundaries are integral to our personal identity and sense of individuality. Without them, we are unable to determine where we end and others begin. We become confused about what actions we have influenced in the world around us. When we believe that we are responsible for our abuse, we have a signal that our internal boundaries have been damaged or need some development. Internal boundaries allow us to let go of things that are not our responsibility—our abuse, other people's actions, the weather. Internal boundaries also help us hold on to our self-worth. As we develop healthy internal boundaries, we grow in our self-esteem. We are able to let go of unnecessary shame and self-blame. We are able to allow others to be responsible for their own actions.

To test your internal boundaries, ask yourself: Do I feel like an individual, separate from others? Am I able to examine and release responsibility for things that have nothing to do with me? Do I feel responsible for the abuse that happened to me or others? Do I feel guilty when something beyond my control upsets a friend or family member? Am I able to see myself as a person apart from my spouse, partner, best friend?

If you sense that you need to work further on developing your boundaries, do the following exercises or ask your therapist to assist you.

EXERCISES FOR DEVELOPING BOUNDARIES

1. As you go through the day, observe how you feel moving among other people. Do you feel differently depending on how close or how far away someone is? Test this by imagining narrowing the space between you and a coworker, a friend, a stranger. In each case, at what distance is your comfort level disturbed? Keep track of the physical distances at which you are comfortable. They are part of your physical boundaries.

2. Practice saying no. Pick a safe person and setting and ask the person to make requests of you. Then practice saying no. "Can I give you a hug?" "Would you make some coffee?" "Will you rub my back?" "I know you are eating, but can you talk to me on the phone?"

3. Draw a picture or a chart of your boundaries, external and internal. To help you visualize your boundaries, place the names of various people where they fit on the chart in relation to you. Are the boundaries soft or hard? Thick, thin, or in between? Are there places that need extra layers of boundaries?

4. Close your eyes and imagine that you are surrounded by a bubble. Breathe deeply. The bubble is invisible to everyone but you. It is permeable, allowing light, air, and sound to pass in and out. But within the bubble are you and your space. Imagine the bubble around you. Touch it and see how it feels. Observe its position in relation to you.

   Now imagine a person outside of your bubble. This person says something to you, and the words enter your bubble. Hold the words in your hand and see what they say. Do they belong inside your bubble? If they do not, send them back outside.

   Now, slowly come back to where you are. But leave the bubble in place. Whenever you are disturbed, look to see whether something is inside the bubble that does not belong to you, and let it pass through and away from you. When you are uncomfortable, imagine yourself inside the bubble. What is it that is disturbing you? Is there something inside your bubble that does not belong there? If there is, let go of it and send it outside the bubble. Then breathe deeply and imagine your bubble healthy and intact.

Disclosures

The process of developing friendships and supportive relationships includes evaluating the need for disclosure about our abuse. It is important to have as a part of our support network those who know about our experience and can support us as we work through our healing process. Telling about our abuse and being heard and believed is a validating, healing experience.

It is also important to know when we should not make disclosures about the abuse. Sharing a disclosure can be inappropriate in some settings. And sometimes disclosures can be hurtful or devastating to a friendship or to one's own sense of safety.

Determining the safety and appropriateness of such sharing involves testing the trust level and depth of the relationship and asking whether such a disclosure would cross boundaries. Is the person to whom you would like to disclose someone you know well? Has your relationship developed so that your conversations are mutual and appropriate? Are you at a point in your relationship where you have shared other important things and had them received and heard? Do you sense that this person is trustworthy? Do you have expectations about this person's response to your disclosure? Imagine telling the person about your abuse. How would you and those inside you feel afterwards?

Be aware of your expectations and needs which may be motivating your desire to disclose. Many of us who come from wounded childhoods use disclosures about ourselves to create instant intimacy—it is the only way we know. Is your disclosure the first step toward making your relationship more intimate? If this is the case, slow down for now and build up to talking about the abuse.

Before disclosing, talk over your thoughts with your therapist, helper, or a friend. If you make the decision to disclose about your abuse, think through how much you would like to say and what you need from that person. Decide whether you would like to ask the person to keep the information confidential.

Make a plan for how to maintain internal safety after the disclosure. Telling about the abuse may stir up feelings of confusion, fear, and vulnerability. Be prepared for these feelings, and remind everyone inside that the feelings are about the abuse and that today you are safe.

As you practice making decisions about disclosures and have experiences of safe disclosures, this process will flow more easily.

Remember that you have the right to decide with whom you share and what requests you make about confidentiality. You have a responsibility to protect yourself. In addition, you have the responsibility to take the action to continue your healing.

Building relationships, setting boundaries, and making appropriate disclosures are all a part of that healing journey.

Wendy's Disclosure

I had been going out with this guy for a month or so. I hadn't told him about the abuse yet. He just knew I'd had a bad childhood (understatement of the century). We were driving home from a movie that focused on good and evil in people. The movie was disturbing, and I could tell I was leaving my body as we drove home. I knew I was disturbed because of the movie, but also because it was time for me to tell him about my crazy childhood.

It seemed a good time — dark and in the car so he couldn't look at me. Being hidden—that's my idea of safe. So I blurted it out in my usual fashion of disclosure: Describe it quickly and in as few sentences as possible. Like diving into a cold swimming pool. There was a long silence after I spoke. I like it when I tell people and they *immediately* say how sorry they are and how terrible that must have been and how mad they are at my parents. I don't like it when they don't say anything. I feel like I'm being judged in that silence.

So I asked him if I had freaked him out. He said I had. Great. I felt like a weirdo. Then he said the worst thing anyone can say: "Are you sure?"

What did he think? I was just making up this stuff to add spice to my life? Of course I also felt like I shouldn't have told him because I upset him. If it upset him to hear it described in three sentences, think how it felt being in my life for twenty years! At least I didn't worry too long about hurting his feelings—I moved right on to anger. I was glad to get home and away from him. If people can't handle it, then I don't want them in my life. Healing is a big part of my life, and I need all the support I can get.

GETTING A NEGATIVE REACTION

We can prepare ourselves for a disclosure, but we cannot control the response of the other person. Most of the time, if we listen to our inner wisdom and think through the step with others, our disclosures turn out fine. But sometimes we may receive a negative reaction.

People may say they do not believe us. They may pretend they did not hear what we said. They may change the subject. Or they may indicate, verbally or nonverbally, that they never want to hear about this again.

If something like this happens, it is most important to remember that their response is not about you. Their response is about them! It is about their own woundedness, life circumstance, insecurity, or the like. Their response does not say anything about you and your value, the truth about your abuse, etc.

Call a friend and talk about what happened. Do something nurturing for yourself. Process your feelings about what happened and be aware of any negative internal messages that may be triggered by the experience.

Such experiences are uncomfortable and painful. And they are normal. But they are occurrences that we can learn from and add to our list of life experiences. Remember that you are a valuable and courageous survivor. Building networks of support, defining boundaries, and making disclosures are hard work and life-giving work.

THINKING THROUGH A DISCLOSURE

1. What about this person? Is he or she safe? trustworthy? Have you established some depth of relationship before now?
2. Would a disclosure be appropriate given the boundaries you have established with this person? Is the relationship mutual (where both persons share relatively equally)? Is a disclosure appropriate in the setting in which you have this relationship? (Is this a work relationship? a friendship?)
3. Have you talked this over with someone? your therapist? another survivor?
4. Do you feel safe internally with this person? Does this person feel trustworthy to everyone inside? Have you listened to your inner wisdom?
5. What is your safety plan? How will you take care of yourself if you are upset after the disclosure? If there is a negative response to the disclosure?
6. Write out the steps of the safety plan.

Michelle's Story

Michelle is a survivor of satanic ritual abuse who is an ordained United Methodist clergyperson. She specializes in youth ministry and counseling. The combination of psychotherapy and spirituality has freed her from the chains of the past. Now Michelle wants to assist others in utilizing the gift of their faith to enable their own growth and healing.

As I write this, I am on vacation, relaxing by the ocean. It is nothing short of a miracle that I can say "relaxing," because until recently, I don't believe I was ever able to relax. On the outside I appeared to be a fun, "all-together" professional woman, but inside I was a mess. I had been secretly bulimic for over sixteen years. I tried cross-country running in an effort to work out all the inner rage, turmoil, and pain. Yet it was to no avail; I still had horrible nightmares, and I struggled through each day.

My first step on the road to recovery began when I checked myself into a treatment center that deals especially with eating disorders. In the course of therapy, I began to have body memories and flashbacks. I began to realize that I had been sexually abused as a child. The trauma and pain of the childhood abuse had been so deep that I carried no adult recollections. I had buried the memories deep in the crevasses of my being, medicating through the bulimia.

This realization of abuse was painful. In treatment, I learned to grieve, to vent rage and anger, and to cry deeply from the bottom of my heart. I began to have some understanding of why my internal life was so chaotic.

After leaving treatment, I continued some of the skills I learned there: writing, journaling, and drawing. But I fell in love with drawing. They were little kid's pictures, but it felt cathartic to just sit and draw whatever came into my head.

I drew more and more. Pretty soon the pictures began turning violent and ugly. I had no clue where these pictures of horrific things were coming from. I only continued to draw and draw.

Concurrently, my life began to fall apart again. I felt like I was losing control. I was barely functioning at work and my bulimia began again. My nights became so scary that I hated having to sleep.

I needed to enter the treatment center again. Once there, I really seemed to fall apart. I fought the rules, began hurting myself, continued my bulimia, and became exhausted from the stress. The staff helped me to shut down and calm my inner intensity enough so that I could function on the outside.

After leaving the center, I continued to draw my pictures. I took my pictures to each therapy session and showed them to Mary (my therapist). In the sessions I cried, vented rage and hatred at my family. And still I wasn't sure what all these pictures were about, at least I wasn't sure enough to talk about it.

The Realizations

I knew there was something there that I wasn't naming. After reading in a sexual abuse recovery book about symptoms of satanic ritual abuse, the realization finally hit. I took all my drawings to my next session with Mary, and uttered in tears, "Mary, this is me. I was ritually abused."

The realization for Mary had dawned months earlier, yet she waited for my own self-discovery. As I proceeded with therapy, emotions seemed to intensify. I began self-mutilative behaviors, my bulimia intensified, and certain times of the year I seemed to get worse. (What I now know is that I was hitting programming head on. I was programmed to hurt myself and to be in pain if I revealed the truth of what happened to me.) Some of the inner intensity was alleviated in my therapy sessions as I cried and slowly let out memories.

I noticed in my journaling that I had all sorts of different types of handwriting. In therapy sessions, I curled up in a ball and had the voice of kids. My next realization was that I have MPD. Now I really wanted to freak out. I am a sane, all-together, fun-loving, professional woman. I'm not crazy!

Well, as my therapy has continued, I have come to realize that being a multiple is a gift. Had I not become multiple, I probably would not have survived the abuse. Each time I faced a horrible ritual, I built up a wall around it and froze that memory in time. Each "child" who developed helped contain some horrible incident and enabled me to survive by not having to remember the event.

The Retreat

The next phase of my recovery involved meeting Gwen, a therapist who uses Christian ritual and imagery to replace and undo what was done to me in satanic ritual. I went on a retreat that Gwen led. I felt skeptical and wary—my mother and stepfather (who are among my abusers) are fundamentalist, charismatic Christians. I would not go for any hokey stuff.

As we survivors sat in a group, Gwen worked with one person at a time. My "parts" (or kids, as I now call them) began to trust her. On Friday night we allowed Gwen to work with us. I was feeling totally defenseless against my family. Gwen helped me envision my Higher Power (whom I call Christ) sitting with me and even hugging me. A part inside of me that hated me and wanted to kill me tried to put up a fight. But we used the power of God to silence this part and then hold, care for, and even heal her. We discovered that behind all this rage and hatred was a programmed, little five-year-old.

Peeling the Onion

It is hard to explain, but for the first time in many months, I felt at peace within. I felt free for the first time; able to relax, concentrate, and work.

After returning from the retreat, my therapist was pleasantly astounded at the change within me. I had reached another layer of my healing. My therapy was like peeling an onion. The more I peeled, the more tears I shed. It was as though my body had built a defense system that enabled me to start with the less horrible of my memories and gradually work deeper into the more painful ones.

Even with my newfound spirituality and self-care skills, the reality became incredibly painful as I went deeper. I was trying to maintain two lives—that of a professional woman and that of a woman undergoing incredibly painful therapy. So I decided to take one month off and focus just on therapy to allow myself the freedom and space to work on my inner self. I went to a treatment center that had expertise in working with survivors of satanic ritual abuse.

During this time, I learned to work with my inner kids. I was still somewhat embarrassed and ashamed by them. I learned that it was not only okay to let the kids out, but it was necessary in order to heal. The kids are the ones with the memories.

At treatment I utilized the twelve-step tradition in my recovery. Parts of me use my faith to help me through. Some parts of me are triggered by Christianity, but other parts of me are able to accept and reclaim my faith. And, in a strange way, my faith is encouraged by the reality of the abuse. If God (and for me, Christ) were not a reality, then why would satanism have been created?

Continuing to Heal

It has been over two years since I last went to treatment. My healing continues one day at a time. I see or call Gwen a few times a year when layers are uncovered that need the power of God for healing, or when I find spiritual strangleholds that need to be broken through. I see Mary weekly and allow all my kids to work as they need. Because of Mary's availability, genuine concern, and caring, I have learned to trust. I am able to risk letting out the deepest of my vulnerabilities and scared little kids. Because of her nurturing, I am learning to nurture my own kids.

I take time for me and my kids. I continue to draw, journal, and play. Play is an essential, therapeutic part of life. The more I learn to recapture my sense of play and my sense of trust that my Higher Power loves me, the more at peace I am with myself and the world.

People made choices to hurt me severely. But I believe that God was there weeping at each incident. Because God has shown me love through other people, especially Mary, I have been able to feel God's loving arms enfolding me, granting me hope, strength, and courage. I see God working through this horrendous situation of my past by using me to help others. I can show others that they too can survive.

Early in my recovery, I learned the motto "Trust the process." As I have learned to trust the process of letting go, letting my kids out, allowing others to help me, trusting Mary, and allowing my Higher Power to heal me, I have made miraculous strides in healing.

CHAPTER FOUR

Kid Management

I like to eat ice cream. / I like to climb trees. / I like to jump in piles of leaves. / But I REALLY like to fly. / When I fly, no one can see me. / When I fly, I float upside down. / When I fly, I go higher than the trees. / And I never fall down.

—Ellie and Lisa, ages three and four

Creative Survival

Often one of the most challenging, irritating, exciting, and confusing things about the process of uncovering ritual abuse is the discovery that there are vast parts of yourself that you do not know. That where you thought you knew all about yourself, you discover that there are large chunks of your history of which you have no knowledge. And further, for many of us, that there are more parts of us than we knew we had. You will hear many terms to describe these phenomena—selective amnesia, splitting, dissociative identity disorder, posttraumatic stress disorder, inner child, or inner children. I call these reactions to trauma "creative survival" and "kid management."

Each person responds to and copes with trauma in different ways. Because our emotions, our environment, our psychological responses, our physical makeup are different, we respond to external stimuli (such as abuse) in different ways. Some people "forget" their abuse; others do not. Some people develop other parts to carry the abuse; others do not. You have your own coping skills which helped you survive what happened to you. As you heal, you will learn what these coping skills are. Whether or not you have developed many selves within, it may be helpful to your healing process to learn about managing the child parts, the wounded parts within you. If this section of the book is scary or new to you, that's okay. Talk with someone about how you feel. And remember that all of these reactions to trauma are normal, creative, and courageous.

The Clinical Labels: Information and Definitions

In the first chapter of the book, I talked briefly about the psychological process that happens when people experience trauma. To review: When trauma occurs that is too great for a person to handle (sexual or physical abuse, a car accident, a natural disaster), the brain takes care of the person by creating an amnesic barrier around the part of the brain where that information is stored. These memories, surrounded by amnesic barriers, can be called "trauma pockets." When these types of memories break through the amnesic barriers, the survivor will have no prior memory of the event that is being recalled. The events were encapsulated completely and were stored in the brain so that the daily, functioning self has no access to them.

It is not known what causes these amnesic barriers finally to be broken open. For some people, present life events may cause the old information to finally break through. My memories began breaking through after a combination of life events: I was in a stable place in my life, good job, place to live, network of friends and family; I was taking good care of myself, having worked hard to overcome some destructive habits; and my niece was born, the first child of the next generation. I was safe, stable, and strong enough to handle the information, so the information came.

POSTTRAUMATIC STRESS DISORDER

The treatment model that works well for many survivors is based on the work that has been done with persons who have posttraumatic stress disorder (PTSD). PTSD is the development of symptoms such as flashbacks, exaggerated startle response, sleep disorders, etc., following a dramatic, psychologically distressing event. (See appendix A for a detailed description of PTSD.)

This PTSD treatment model (developed in response to work with combat veterans) assumes that the emotional and behavioral defenses to the trauma (repression, dissociation, medicating through various addictions, hypervigilance, development of fragments or distinct personalities in addition to the primary personality) are normal, creative, and healthy responses to the horror of the trauma. In this model, the goals of treatment are recognition, acceptance, and integration of the trauma.

(Traditional treatment models see the emotional and behavioral defenses as problems to be treated rather than signs of trauma and/ or signs that a person is healing. Therefore, the person is labeled sick, psychotic, delusional, or the like and is treated to alleviate symptoms rather than to address the source of the symptoms. The treatment has traditionally included invasive methods such as drug therapy or shock treatments.)

In the PTSD model, phenomena such as flashbacks, somatization, and dissociation are signs that the person is experiencing a normal reaction to a trauma. The emphasis is on learning to work with the self to gain the skills needed to reach the goals of functioning in health and integrating the new memories into one's life.

DISSOCIATIVE IDENTITY DISORDER

When the abuse is severe, repetitive, and occurs over a long period of time, survivors may develop coping skills clinically defined as dissociative identity disorder (DID). (In 1994, the American Psychiatric Association changed the name from multiple personality disorder [MPD] to dissociative identity disorder [DID]. See appendix A for detailed definitions.) These coping skills are on one end of a scale of reactions to trauma that Ray Giles describes as "going from bad to bad."[1] That is, all trauma is bad. People cope with it in different ways.

Dissociation is the same thing as "spacing out." It is something that everyone does. (Do you ever recall driving home from work and not remembering a portion of the trip because you were thinking about something else? That's dissociation.) Survivors of abuse—all kinds of abuse—frequently develop the skill of dissociation as a protective measure against the abuse. Children dissociate, leave their bodies, go somewhere else, become a part of the pattern in the wallpaper, or fly to their favorite outdoor spot.

When the abuse is frequent and very severe, as in ritual abuse, the dissociation is more extensive and the areas of the brain containing the trauma become more developed or more numerous. When one part of a child has received repeated abuse over a long period of time, then that part goes through developmental stages and actually becomes another—sometimes fully functioning—part of that individual. That other part of a person is called an "alter" (the clinical term is *alter personality*).

Dissociative identity disorder and *multiple personality disorder* are the terms clinicians use to describe when parts of the brain were developed in response to the trauma. Responses to trauma are very different depending on many factors, so there is much variety in the way people manifest dissociative disorders. A diagnosis of dissociative identity disorder has to do with how well developed the parts or alters are and whether there are "two or more distinct identities or personality states."[2] The presence of partially developed personality fragments, rather than distinct identities, is often diagnosed as *dissociative disorder not otherwise specified* (DDNOS).

Some people with a dissociative disorder have numerous parts or fragments of parts with which they are co-conscious. The adult or primary part of the person (host personality) is aware of when the other parts are out and may have varying abilities to talk to or influence these parts.

Some survivors have fully functioning alters with whom they are not co-conscious. These alter personalities may perform various functions in the person's life, such as going to work, getting up in the morning, attending social events. Persons may have many different distinct parts which are all a part of them and which are results of the trauma.

Alters may or may not be aware of each other. They may be any age, gender, race, or sexual orientation. They may have names.

In the PTSD treatment model, the goal for persons with dissociative disorders is to get all of the fragments and parts functioning as a unit. If the adult part of the person is not present when the other parts come out, then the first goal is to help the adult learn to communicate with the parts within. If co-consciousness is already present, then the goal is to get the various parts to work together in union.

A NOTE ABOUT INTEGRATION

Many helpers from the psychiatric community see integration as the goal of treatment for persons with multiple personality disorder. Integration is defined as "the process of bringing together the separate thought processes (personalities or fragments) and maintaining them as one."[3]

This notion of integration is very disturbing to some persons with multiplicity. One survivor said that it was upsetting to think of losing the richness of the many alters she had discovered in her process of healing. The key to this dilemma is that all survivors have within them their own paths to health. Integration as defined above may not be the right answer for some survivors. For others, integration may be the specific piece that sets them free. Each one must find the way that is right for her or him. The system holds all the wisdom and creativity needed to make this decision. It is to be hoped that psychiatrists and other helpers will be supporters of each person's process.

Creative Survival versus Labels

When we begin to uncover memories of ritual abuse *and* discover that we may have some inner parts that resulted from the abuse, many of us feel shame, anger, or resistance at being labeled as having "dissociative identity disorder," "multiple personality disorder," or "dissociative disorder not otherwise specified." It sounds pretty serious, pretty clinical, pretty crazy. But in actuality, what is serious and crazy is the abuse that we survived!

When the medical community labels us as having a "disorder" it is quite a shock. When we are labeled rather than naming ourselves, those who create the labels have the power.

We have choice about how we respond to the labeling. We can see ourselves as "disordered," or we can see our multiplicity as creative survival. *Multiplicity* is a term being used by survivors to describe their creative survival. We can choose to name ourselves, our strengths, and our powers to heal.

It is important to realize that for those of us who have many parts, becoming aware of our multiplicity is a sign that we are beginning to heal. Many parts first surface with a memory of abuse. They are carriers of our abuse, our feelings, our childhood. As we become a larger and larger family of adult and inner children, we are regaining parts of ourselves that the abuse took away from us. We are recovering our wholeness of being. We are reclaiming or discovering for the first time who we really are, in all its diversity. One survivor said that for her, the best part of uncovering her ritual abuse was finding all the parts within and the many gifts that they brought to her life.

So whatever you choose to call it for yourself, you are a strong, creative, innovative survivor of ritual abuse. You—we—are some of the strongest people on earth because of our creative survival. We may not have survived had we not developed the ability to dissociate. Honor your gifts of survival and your ability to heal from profound wounds.

The Process of Discovery

The process of discovering whether there are other parts within is different for every survivor. Some survivors find many different parts within—of all different ages, genders, and experiences. Other survivors discover one child within, the wounded one who took all of the abuse. Some survivors may not discover separate parts of themselves. Each way of coping is okay; and whatever is true for you is just right. The process is unique because you, your brain, your personality, your response to outside events are all unique.

There are many ways to explore the parts inside of us. Some of us discover our inner selves as we work through the process of recovering memories of abuse. Planned regressions or spontaneous flashbacks may bring us to an inner place where we meet one or more parts of us that we have not met before. We may encounter a five-year-old who carries lots of anger. Or we may meet a very frightened, withdrawn seven-year-old. We may discover a thirteen-year-old part of us who courageously lived through abuse.

Some of us discover other parts of us when we realize that we are not always the one functioning in all the areas of our life. We may gradually realize that someone else buys the groceries, goes to work, or gets ready in the morning. We may discover that there are various parts of us who have other tastes in clothes or food.

Sometimes we hear voices talking within us, or we have the sense that we are "we" rather than "I." Sometimes, in the middle of reality, we see the scene as though we were miles away or as though we were observing it, rather than really being there.

Many of us discover other parts, other voices, when we journal, do creative writing, or draw. One technique that allows selves within to come forward is to draw or write using our nondominant hand (the hand we usually do *not* use to write). For example, create a dialogue by using your dominant hand to talk for your adult, primary self. Then, using your other hand, write what comes—do not censor it. This technique allows other parts of us to talk with us.

Frederick Buechner, a writer and theologian, describes his use of this technique: "My right hand is my grown-up hand ... but when I wrote with the left hand, I found that what tended to come out was as artless and basic as the awkward scrawl it came out in. It was as if some of my secrets had at last found a way of communicating with me directly."[4]

Use your other hand to write about events from your childhood. Or draw pictures of your memories. We glean much information as we ask questions and listen to the answers of the various parts of us. This process of discovery is sometimes strange, a little bit scary, funny, unusual, rewarding, and unique. It is a process of discovering our wholeness.

WHO ARE THEY?

Who are the parts within? They are children, teenagers, young adults, older adults. They are male and female, straight and gay, asexual and confused. They are all shapes, sizes, colors, and religions. They are mean and hateful, and sweet and gentle. They are addicts and abusers. They are victims and protectors. All are survivors who helped you get through your abuse.

Clinicians have created labels to describe some types of alters: persecutor, host, internal helper, gatekeeper, protector. These names describe functional alters that clinicians have observed in people with whom they have worked.

But for many of us, discovering the kids or alters within is much richer and more colorful than these labels indicate. Some of the parts within are innocent and childlike. These little ones may be very easy to meet, to work with, to take care of.

Other alters may carry strong identification with the abusers. They may be "children of the dark side." They may indicate that they are still part of the cult or that they intend to carry on abuse activities. They may bring threats against themselves, you, or others. These alters may have been created by the abusers as a part of the abuse to carry messages and values of the perpetrators. (See chapter 5, on reprogramming.) Or they may be speaking in the only language they know—threats and hatred.

Some alters have designated jobs to do. You can find out if they have a job by asking them. If their job is destructive or unsafe, you can negotiate with them to take a new job. They will often switch jobs if you can agree on one of equal or greater importance.

Most of these destructive alters are just very wounded children and young people. However, it is very important to deal with them when they present themselves. (For suggestions on this, refer to the section on "Creative Problem Solving" later in this chapter.) Ask for help from your therapist or helper. It is often difficult for survivors to handle these alters by themselves. As you peel back the layers of hate, bravado, and woundedness, you will find ways to work with these angry, sometimes difficult, alters. And underneath, you will find some of your strongest internal allies and protectors.

All of these inner ones—the innocent children, the destructive teenagers, and the wise old people—are creative and valuable. Each of them, in his or her own way, helped you to survive until today.

CULTIVATING COMMUNICATION

Drawing, coloring, painting, and journaling using your nondominant hand are all ways to allow the selves within to express themselves and communicate with you. Try coloring outside the lines in a coloring book. Try finger painting. Try stream-of-consciousness writing. Don't censor or analyze anything that comes. Over time, you may become aware that ages of you are emerging. Make a commitment to listen for one-half hour every day to the parts within. It is very important for you to listen and believe the ones who choose to communicate with you. By opening communication, you have invited them into your life. Your job as parent/adult is to listen, believe, be there for them, and be nonjudgmental.

System Management: The Family Model

System is the word used to describe the whole of us, our self made up of many parts. The goal of healing is to get all the parts of us functioning as a unit. With our many parts, we are a network of individual pieces that relate and function more or less as a whole. Many times, when we begin to heal, we do not function as a whole very well. The word *system* is a helpful descriptor for this goal of healing, because it connotes parts working together, communicating, and relating to each other.

You are the one who is in charge of your healing. You are the one in charge of your system. As the one with the responsibility, you have the option to choose the methods of healing that are best for you and your system. There are many helpful and valid models and methods of healing.

I cannot outline here all of the models of healing and system management. But I can share what has worked for me and my system. My model of healing may not be the right way for you. You will find the way that works best for you.

The model of system management that works best for me is a family model, where the inner parts are grouped together by age. We attempt to function as a healthy system with me as the "parent" or "coordinator." Different parts relate to me in different ways, but I am the one who is in charge and who takes care of all the alters. The style of management I use is a parenting model. In our system, the parts or alters prefer to be called "the kids."

Your system may not work as a family. Your alters may not want to be called kids. You may have a corporate model, a consensus model, an extended community model. The model does not matter, as long as it works for you. Use your knowledge and your creativity to see what model fits for you and your system. Talk with other survivors to find out what works for them. What matters is that you learn to function together as a whole in life-giving, healthy ways.

Much of this chapter is based on experiences using the family model for system management. Even if your system functions with a different style of management, some of these techniques may be helpful to you. Adapt or create your own techniques for system management.

DEVELOPING PARENTING SKILLS

I use the descriptor "inner kids" or "inner children" to describe these various parts or alters that were created by the abuse. After all, they are, most of them, just kids. For many of us, these new parts of ourselves may be the first children we have had to parent. Or, if we are the parents of biological or adopted children, we may have parented two or three or five children—but not ten or fifty or one hundred! The parts within can range in age from infant to elderly, but the ones who need the most parenting, the most management, are the children, preteens, and teenagers. Sure, they are not real, biological kids. But they are real. And an inner three-year-old can be as scared or mad as an "outer" three-year-old. An inner fifteen-year-old can be as crafty or devious as an "outer" fifteen-year-old.

For us new parents learning to manage our inner selves, learning parenting skills is a priority. I call this part "kid management."

As a new parent, you may be feeling overwhelmed, confused about your role, unsure of how to parent an inner brood. Parenting inner kids is much like parenting "outer" kids, except that with inner kids you are the only one who can hear them screaming or crying all at once. On the other hand, inner kids are cheaper to take to a movie or out to eat. And you don't have to change diapers or pay a baby-sitter.

Since we abuse survivors did not grow up in functional homes, we probably did not learn healthy parenting from our parents. We can learn parenting skills today from a variety of sources. Our therapists and helpers may model for us good parenting skills as they work with us. We can observe the behavior of parents who grew up in more functional homes or who have learned healthy ways to parent. We can ask lots of questions or read books on raising children. The goal is to have safety, a modicum of manageability, and a life that is growing in healing.

Often we discover inner kids at the same time as we discover ritual abuse. Many times, we meet kids as they break into our consciousness with a memory of abuse. The early days of remembering and parenting are quite difficult. It is okay to do the best you can and learn from your mistakes. (That is actually how most parents of biological children learn to be good parents.)

The rest of the chapter will give you some hints and beginning places on the journey to parenting the inner children.

IMAGINATION AS A HELPING TOOL

Imagination is one of the most powerful tools for healing that we have. It is one of the gifts that kept us alive as children. We were able to dissociate, change identities, pretend that what was happening was not happening, fly away from the abuse, become too tiny to be seen, or even disappear. That same imagination can help us heal today, especially as we work with our inner children.

Some of us have always used imagination as a tool in our lives. Others of us may feel as though we have lost our ability to imagine, to pretend. Some of us have used logic, realism, and analytic thinking to cope with our abuse. If that is the case, we may think that imagination is for kids and that this "inner child stuff" is made up and childish. It is hard to trust the process and believe the things we are remembering. Imagination, along with its companion, creativity, is not only the possession of children. It is a powerful healing tool for our abuse.

CREATING A SAFE PLACE

One of the first and most important steps in managing the new family is being sure that the kids have a safe place to live. Even before we know who they are, we can create a safe place for them to live. We are now, whether we like it or not, responsible to care for them. We may not have chosen the abuse or the recovery from the abuse or the many kids within us, but the kids are a part of us and a part of our healing.

Your therapist can help you create a safe place through a guided imagery. This place may be a castle surrounded by a moat, a cottage by a clear stream in the mountains, a horse ranch in the west, a village in another country, a hidden meadow with beautiful flowers. The safe place may include protectors to watch over the children. You are the only one who can enter the safe place. The kids are totally safe and cannot be harmed. At the safe place, they can live and play and be children—some of them for the first time. They can meet the other children who are a part of the family, get to know each other, and learn to work together.

Your safe place should feel safe and be safe. You can create whatever you need to make it a safe place for the kids to live. It can be fun; a nice place for kids to live. Let the kids draw a picture of the safe place and all the toys they would like to have there. You can bring in as many inner helpers as you need to take care of the family. If you like, you can have your therapist or other helpers live there and assist in the care of the kids.

If you have difficulty imagining and creating a safe place for the kids, do the guided imagery in appendix B.

TEN SUGGESTIONS FOR NEW PARENTS

1. *Spend time with the kids and get to know them.* Find out how old they are, their names, what they like to do, who else they know in the system, what their jobs are/were. If you want to, draw map of your system.

2. *Make a kids' book.* Use a loose-leaf binder with a divider for each child. Let each kid draw a picture of him/herself, or cut and paste from a magazine a picture that looks like him or her. Use the book to record dialogues with the kids, memories, conversations with God, wish lists, etc. Have the kids help decorate

the outside of the binder. (If the kids are willing to share, this binder can be a big help to your therapist when he or she wants to get to know the kids.)

3. *Think through your role in the system.* Are you willing to be a parent? (Do the kids want you as a parent?) Are you the system coordinator or manager? Explore what role feels most comfortable to both you and the kids. (In my system, I am parent to the younger kids and coordinator to the older kids.)

4. *Make a tape of you talking to the kids and/or ask your therapist to make a tape.* On the tape, greet the kids by name and give positive messages. Say the things the kids might need to hear during a crisis or at a time when you are too worn out to take care of them. Play the tape when the kids are needing comfort, nurture, or calming.

5. *Build a support network of other adults you can call on.* Select people you can trust and ask them if they can be available to give extra help with the kids if you need it. (Single parenting is *hard work!*) Tell your support people about what you need and do not need at such times. (Example: "I need someone to listen to my five-year-old. I do not need you to fix me.")

6. *Schedule regular parenting breaks.* Take a break for a weekend and send all the kids camping (or to the ocean, the amusement park, the zoo, space camp, etc.). Send along plenty of your (or their) favorite inner adult helpers or therapists. Tell them they can be in touch with you and you with them by remote video at any time, but their job is to have fun and your job is to rest.

7. *Educate yourself about age-level development.* (See the age-level development chart below and the resources section at the end of this book.) Learn about how kids of different ages handle grief, anger, death, etc. Learn age-appropriate sexuality and how to parent children who have been wounded.

8. *Find out what you—the adult—like to do, and take time to do it.* Develop that adult part of you and spend time with yourself. Don't spend all your time doing what the kids want to do. Get a baby-sitter or take a parenting break if you need to.

9. *Learn to say no to the kids.* (You can practice this with your therapist, your helpers, or another parent.) "No, you cannot come
    out at work." "No, you cannot cut or harm me." "No, you can-
   not drive the car." Set boundaries, limits, and guidelines to keep
   everybody safe. Children (even inner ones) need and want limits to help them feel safe.

10. *Allow yourself to make mistakes.* Parenting is a learning process.
    One important way we learn is through making mistakes. Mak-
    ing mistakes doesn't mean you are a bad parent (all parents learn
    this way). If you make a mistake that causes harm to the kids,
    make amends to them as soon as you realize it. Say you are
    sorry, that you did not intend to hurt them, that you will do it
    differently the next time. In this way, you are modeling healthy,
    mature behavior for the kids.

Basic Management Skills

One of the most challenging parenting skills is learning the appropriate situations in which child alters can be out and those in
which the adult/parent needs to be in charge and the kids put
away.

As the parent/adult, you set the rules for the system about where
and when the kids can be out. Children do not need to be at work,
figuring out family finances, having sex, or participating in other
adult tasks. It is up to the parent to take responsibility for setting
these rules and helping everyone inside stick to them.

WHAT IF I DON'T HAVE AN ADULT?

Some of us come into this process wondering whether or not we
even have an adult. It is obvious that we have been able to cope
well enough to survive in the world, but is there really a part of us

that has functioned in the world as an adult? Or have various parts functioned as adults by using our creative coping skills?

This is a recurring question for many of us in our recovery. Sometimes it is impossible to answer.

But it is time now to begin to develop whatever parent/adult skills we have into a mature, responsible, functioning adult. Make a list of the characteristics of your ideal parent/adult. This list will reflect the values and skills that you might want to develop in your adult/parent self.

Some qualities might include compassion, ability to take responsibility, good boundaries, assertiveness, ability to detach, and nurturing skills.

EXERCISE FOR DEVELOPING AN ADULT

1. Pick an adult activity with a specific time limit and schedule a time to do it. (Examples: Going to a lecture, visiting a friend, attending a twelve-step meeting, group therapy, etc.)
2. Before you begin the activity, quiet yourself and imagine all the inner parts younger than your biological age going to their safe place. Imagine yourself standing alone as an adult.
3. During the activity at the scheduled time, check in with yourself every five to fifteen minutes to see if you are still in your adult and if the kids are still in their safe place. If not, take time and repeat Step 2.
4. Try to be fully present with your activity, hearing and seeing all that is happening in the moment.
5. At the end of the activity or time that you specified, thank the inner parts for their cooperation and evaluate the exercise. Were you able to stay present in the activity? Were you able to stay in your adult? How did it feel? Was it a new or a familiar experience? What were the things that helped or hindered your ability to stay in your adult?

Age-Level Development[5]

Age-Level	Characteristics / Task	Understanding of Death	Faith Issues	Parental Role
Infancy & toddler, 0–2	Development of trust, early emotional development. Differentiation of self from the environment.	No concept of death.	Development of trust, courage, hope, and love.	Provide quality and consistency of care.
Preschool, 2–6	First self-awareness. Magical/fantasy thinking. Lack of reasoning skills. Need for affection. Development of language, sex-role identification, self-control, and early moral development.	View death as reversible. Illness and death seen as punishments for child's bad thoughts or actions.	Need for acceptance, stability and security, positive role models. Abundance of questions. Expansion of fantasy to fill the gap between fact and fantasy. Inability to understand symbolism. Need for assurance that God is present and trustworthy even if parents are not. Importance of stories.	Provide protection. Inability to shelter children from grim reality, but ability to provide stories and images that help develop trust, courage, and hope.
School age, 6–10	Expansion of life experiences beyond family. Development of concrete thinking. Abundance of fears and worries. Importance of friendships. Distinct rule-orientation.	Understanding of death's finality. Play acting about death. Personification of death. Greatest death anxiety of any stage. Identification of death as a retaliation for wrong doing.	Interpretation of symbols as literal. Adoption of beliefs, stories from community.	Encouragement, presentation of opportunities for learning and growth.

Age-Level	Characteristics / Task	Understand-ing of Death	Faith Issues	Parental Role
Preadolescence, 10–12	Vulnerability to the lures of mass culture. Importance of fitting in. Development of friendship network. Increasing importance of negotiation in home life. Acute sense of right and wrong.	Understanding of biological process of death. Identification of death as punishment. Death not personified but seen as sad, evil. Practical questions about death.	Interpretation of symbols as literal. Adoption of beliefs, stories from community.	Continue to do things with the preadolescent. Engage in one-on-one shared activities. Demonstrate both firmness and connection. Show your real feelings and admit your mistakes.
Adolescence, 12–18	Physical maturation; concern about bodies. Intricate social network. Disconnection with parents and creation of own identity. Well-developed cognitive skills. Future-orientation. Search for meaning in life.	View of death as inevitable and universal. Identification of death as natural enemy to self. Philosophical thinking. Possible withdrawal or denial of a loss when death occurs.	Faith as a basis for developing values. Faith as a source of structure and ideology.	Support of youth in building their identity. Consistency and realism.

KNOWING WHEN THE KIDS ARE OUT

One of the great challenges of parenting inner children is knowing when they are out. If we don't know when they are out, we cannot parent them appropriately.

Each of us differs in our system make-up, our number of inner parts, our kids' knowledge of each other, our level of co-consciousness with the kids, and our inner parts' distinctiveness and development.

These factors may make it difficult to know who is out and what is going on. Some kids are so distinct that when they are out there is very little or no adult presence. Other times, several kids may be out at the same time as the adult. And sometimes, kids pop out and take over at inappropriate times.

Kids may get triggered out by an unexpected situation. Or they may slip out because the climate is safe and secure. Or they may be out because your adult/parent is too tired and cannot keep them in. But whatever the reason the kids are out, it is the parent's responsibility to decide whether they should be there or not and to put the kids away if the time is inappropriate.

Knowing when the kids are out is a primary step toward creating a safe life for the whole system. But it takes time to learn to recognize them when they are out. (Remember—they are part of you and have been helping you survive for a long time.)

Here are some signals that point to kids being out:

1. *Feelings:* Are your feelings congruent with the current situation? Often, if they are out of proportion or do not make sense, then you are feeling the kids' feelings and one or more of them may be present. A survivor found himself upset and agitated when he took his real-life children on an outing. He realized that one of his inner kids was jealous and upset. He had to take an inner time-out to talk to that child, put him in a safe place and "be the adult" for his outside kids.

2. *Attitude, demeanor, and language:* Subtle signals, attitudes, demeanor, and language may be evidence of errant kids hanging out where they do not belong. When I begin to pull my hands inside the sleeves of my shirt, I know that my ten-year-old is present. If your adult rarely uses profanity, especially at work, you might be alerted that something is brewing when curse words come out of your mouth. Perhaps some of your kids come out when you dress in a certain way. My three- and four-year-olds tend to come out if I am wearing unmatched colors of socks. (Who dressed me?) Rowdy adolescents may cause you to chomp your gum, drive the car faster than usual, or talk tough and swagger. Learning these signals for your system can be a very helpful way to become aware of when different parts of you are out.

3. *Confusion:* Confusion is a symptom of posttraumatic stress disorder. It can also be a clue that the kids are out and in need of attention. You may be flooded by all kinds of thoughts and feelings during a tense situation. If you are unable to think clearly, pause, go inside, and see what is going on. The kids may be peeking out and adding their opinions to an already confusing situation.

4. *Speech:* Listen to yourself talking. Are you talking like your adult/ parent? Listen to vocal tone, vocabulary, intonation. How old do you sound? (six, ten, seventeen?) Are you stuttering? Become aware of the way that you talk when you are in your adult. Also note the speech patterns of various parts of you so that you can recognize who is present.

5. *Self-destructive thoughts:* Most of us can be sure that if we are having self-destructive thoughts or feelings, our inner kids are involved and need immediate attention from our capable, loving adult. Stop whatever you are doing, pay attention, listen, and get support from another adult. Do not let the thoughts rule you. A memory may need to come out or the kids may be upset and need your attention. Whatever you do, do not act on

self-destructive thoughts. To do so would be to reabuse you and the kids.

WHEN THE KIDS GET TRIGGERED OUT: SALVAGING A CRISIS

So, the kids are out at your job and are wreaking havoc on your insides, your coworkers, your pencils, your dignity. What to do?

1. Take a break from whatever you are doing. If you are with unsafe people, excuse yourself and go to a safe place.
2. Sit down and breathe.
3. If possible, get in touch with a support person, either in person or by phone.
4. Go inside and see what is happening.
5. Tell the kids that you hear that they are afraid, angry, or whatever, but that this is not a safe place for them to be right now. Tell them that you need them to go to their safe place and stay there. Tell them that you will come to their safe place and listen to them at a specified time. Image them in their safe place with their inner helpers taking good care of them. Assure them that you, the adult, will take responsibility for the situation and will take good care of them. Return to the present.
6. Keep your appointment with the kids. Be there at the time you said you would be there.

Note: Sometimes the initiating trigger or the response from the kids is so big that it seems that there is no way to get them put away and get your adult back. Use your outside helpers and do the best you can. Remember that you are a survivor of trauma, that your response makes total sense given what you have lived through. Do the best you can in the situation and learn from it. It takes time to learn the skills of managing kids once they have been freed to be a part of your life. Give yourself positive strokes. You are doing the best you can, and it will be okay.

Disaster at the Office

One Friday morning when I was tired and anxious, I got hit with a surprise trigger that threatened the kids. They thought they were going to be deleted, to be killed. Present in my office were two coworkers—one who knew parts of my story and one who did not. Before I knew what was happening, two new teenagers were out, reacting to the trigger by swearing, kicking the desk, and heaving a chair around.

The coworker who knew my story stayed in my office and helped me to calm down. The other coworker ran to get help.

Within an hour, I was in my supervisor's office receiving a reprimand for inappropriate behavior. I felt stunned, hurt, angry, and shamed. My supervisor did not have a clue about what had happened.

It took lots of time, energy, and adult intervention to bring the situation to a passable solution. My therapist and my doctor were willing to help me navigate the institutional jungle. Nothing was placed in my permanent record, but cleaning up after the catastrophe was not pleasant.

Although my ego was wounded, the situation taught me a lot. My most important learnings were:

1. It is not okay for my kids to hang out at the office.
2. I need to learn the signals of when the kids are getting ready to pop out.
3. When I am tired, I am more vulnerable to triggers and I need to be both more alert and gentler with myself.
4. It is inevitable to make mistakes. In fact, it is normal to make mistakes.

Creative Problem Solving

You and the kids can use imagination and creativity for solving problems in the system today. If you are having trouble with a kid who wants to self-harm or behave inappropriately, talk with that kid and others in the system about other options or solutions. Reaffirm any boundaries or contracts that you have set with your system, and work within those limits to creatively solve the problem.

Work a deal. All of us, kids and adults, need to feel that we have choices. Negotiation with children gives them viable choices and teaches them healthier alternatives. "It's not okay to cut the body. But you can draw a picture of what happened to you to make you want to cut. Or you can wear a band-aid or mark the place with a red magic marker."

"It's not okay to break anything. But it is okay to be angry. Would you like to let your anger out in a safe way? If you could be as mad as you want, what would you do?" *"Break a window."* "No, it's not okay to break things. Is there something else you could do? Would you like to pretend this pillow is a window and hit it with a tennis racket?" Keep talking until you have a deal.

Sometimes other kids may have ideas. Ask the system for help if you get stuck. "Does anyone else have an idea of what to do?"

Remember that these are creative, though wounded, kids. Their main purpose has always been to keep you safe. That is what they are doing now. They just don't understand that today they *are* safe. Nor do they know other ways of acting. You have to teach them alternatives. Affirm their worth even as you set limits. "I know you are doing your job. You are doing it very well. But today, we are safe and you don't have to do this job anymore. Can we find you a new job? What would you like to do?"

Don't forget: The parts within are mostly kids who have never had a chance to be kids.

EXAMPLES OF HEALING, SAFETY, AND COMFORT

One of the strengths we have is the creativity that helped us survive. Today, when we are faced with problems on the inside, we can use this creativity to respond to them. Here are some examples from the experiences of other survivors about how they used imagination to solve internal dilemmas.

- A ritual abuse survivor's inner child shared that she had been burned with cigarettes as a part of the abuse. Red marks surfaced on the survivor's body. The survivor asked the child what she needed to be healed. The child asked the survivor to draw a picture of her in a hospital bed with white sheets, pretty flowers, and a nice nurse. The child was comforted. The red marks on the survivor's body went away.
- Unable to sleep because of fear, an imaginative inner child created a ten-foot electric fence around her room with a thick concrete wall outside the fence. No one could get in. Once this fortress had been imagined, everyone in the system felt safe enough to sleep.
- One survivor sits in a rocking chair holding her bear. She imagines all the kids inside the bear and hugs and rocks and holds them close.
- Many survivors have a symbolic figure of strength, a protector, that lives with their kids: a friendly dragon, castle guards, or even a real person, like Arnold Schwarzenegger. My kids are guarded by a tiger that can fly, overcome any opponent, and is invincible to knives or bullets. Whenever an inner child has a memory of abuse, the tiger comes to the rescue and takes the child to a safe place.

WORKING A DEAL

Negotiation combined with imagination is a powerful tool to use in problem solving. Parents of outside kids learn negotiation early on (to help with bedtime, mealtime, bath time, etc.). Difficult situations with inner kids can be resolved. Do not be fooled by things that look like a dead end; keep looking for creative solutions. Or ask the system for ideas. (Most of the time, someone within will know what to do.) A more positive, healthier option can always be found: Work a deal; find them a new job; offer choices or ask for their suggestions. Keep before you your bottom-line values and rules—that everyone must be safe both inside and outside.

Here are some examples of problem solving done by other survivors:

- A five-year-old girl agrees not to cut in exchange for a piece of gum.
- A teenage boy moves to the light side because he likes the color yellow. (He said, "They don't have colors on the dark side.")
- Angry, destructive teenagers take new jobs: acting as bodyguards for therapists, helping with horses and learning to ride, helping the little kids within the system, working with clay to create things instead of breaking things.
- Sometimes helping other people is the only job important enough to take the place of the important jobs kids had before. The kids have information and experience that no one else has. Helping others is a very important contribution to the system and to the world.
- Music (Bach's *Brandenburg Concertos*) convinces ten tough teenagers that they would rather live on the light side. They had never heard music like that on the dark side. They thought it was *awesome*.
- Some kids need encouragement to live at the safe place. Inner pets—horses, dogs, kittens—are great reasons to live at the safe place. Ask them what they would like to have to play with and provide it. (Playgrounds, toys, music, etc.)
- Arnold Schwarzenegger gives everyone at the safe place karate lessons so they can protect themselves without weapons. (Even imaginary weapons are not allowed at this safe place. Arnold had to turn in his gun.)
- Give kids their own rooms at the safe place and let them decorate them. (You might need to set limits, such as no weapons, no decorations using satanic symbols, or no satanic-triggering music.)

USING IMAGINATION IN A CRISIS OR
UNMANAGEABLE SITUATION

Sometimes we—like parents of real-life kids—do not have the energy, support, or resources to be able to deal safely with a destructive kid: a kid addicted to drugs, a sexually addicted child, a suicidally depressed teenager. It is not a reflection on our ability to parent. Rather, it is testimony to the serious consequences of the abuse. The kids have been greatly hurt. And all parents, at times, need help dealing with their children.

In these crisis situations, imagination can help you find solutions that will keep you safe and functioning. It may keep you from having to hospitalize the whole system (including you).

Sometimes alters come forward with destructiveness that is unmanageable for you and the system. They may think their job is to hurt you. They may be out of control with an addiction. They may be suicidal.

With the help of your therapist or other support person, you may decide to do an intervention on this child and get him or her to a place where others can take care of him or her. This kind of situation is difficult whether the child is inner or outer, but the situation is real and normal, and it is the parent's/adult's responsibility to keep the entire system safe.

Unruly kids can be "sent," temporarily, to treatment centers for detox, to wilderness camp for "problem kids," or to an adolescent mental health facility for a short time until they are stabilized and the adult/parent is ready, safe, and strong enough to deal with them. Use your creativity to search for solutions.

If you decide that you need to do an intervention, your therapist or helper can help. In a guided imagery, go through the steps to take the child, admit her or him to the facility, leave them in the capable hands of the trained staff, let go, and come back.

These are some questions to think through when you are confronted with destructive alters:

1. Can I responsibly care for this child without endangering me, the system, or others?
2. If I cannot, what kind of facility/help does this child need?
3. How will I get him or her there?
4. How often and in what ways will I keep in touch with them and their progress?
5. What are the indicators that will show it is safe for this child or teenager to come back?

Wilderness Camp

 In therapy one day, three new teenage boys presented themselves. As my therapist and I worked with them, we discovered that they were charged with the job of killing me. My reaction was, "Oh, great. Here we go again." I was dealing with a lot in my "today life" and I did not have much extra energy to process a lot of programming. My therapist and I evaluated the situation and decided that perhaps they needed to go somewhere other than the safe place—somewhere more secure—so that I had help in handling them. (We had tried this one time before with another unruly teenager, and it had worked well.)

I had recently heard of a wilderness camp for troubled teens. I decided to send them there. They could hike and work and scream out all of their anger under the care of trained counselors. I imagined the camp sending a bus to my therapist's office. In my mind, I watched them file onto the bus. I talked with the counselor on the bus, telling him their names and why they needed to go to camp.

Then I watched the bus leave and imagined it traveling down the interstate to the camp. It arrived at the camp, and my three boys got off the bus and met their counselors. I came back to my therapist's office, and we processed the experience.

Several months later, the three of them were released from camp and came back to the safe place. Since then they have become important caregivers for some of the younger children. And when another male teenager needed to go to wilderness camp, they volunteered to go with him. They are great guys!

SAFETY IS THE FIRST PRIORITY

Use creativity to help you solve internal problems. But remember that the first priority is your safety and survival. There may be times when imaginative solutions will not keep you safe. You may need the extra security of being in a safe place like a hospital or treatment facility. It may be scary, but listen to the counsel of your therapist and helpers if they believe you need extra help. Or if you know inside that no matter how strong and creative you are, you cannot handle what is happening, tell someone and ask them to help you get to safety.

Summary

Learning to manage is a fundamental goal of healing. The ways we learned to manage as children—dissociation, repression—helped us to stay alive until today. Now we learn the limits of those childhood coping skills, and we must learn new skills in order to thrive. Discovering who we are, valuing ourselves, learning to parent—all these things bring us toward healing our wounded places. These aspects take time to develop. There will be successes and mistakes along the way. But the way is rich with the discovery of each part that makes up who we are today.

Adam's Story

There are moments when everything looks new. And fresh. Scrubbed clean like after a spring rain or a long, hard cry. Sometimes my life looks like that, and the world holds the peace of a child in my heart.

I need you to know my story. I need to tell it. I am a survivor of satanic ritual abuse. This type of abuse is a sadistic and systematic form of torture based on instilling terror through repeated rituals and programming over a long period of time. Because the activities of the cult that abused me were so sick and shocking, it has been very difficult for me to admit that my abuse really happened. I have been trying very hard, for a long time, to deny that I was intentionally terrorized as a child in such a brutal and pointless way. Now the evidence is too great to deny it any longer. And sadly, for the first time in my life, everything about my life finally makes sense—my behaviors, tantrums, addictions, nightmares, flashbacks, fears—everything. What a paradox—such relief and such sorrow in the same breath.

The consequences of this abuse in my life make perfect sense.

Even after ten apparently wonderful years of growth and recovery in AA, I felt incredible isolation and inability to trust others.

Naming the Abuse

Naming my abuse was the key to opening the door of hope and freedom. It was one of the most significant events of my life. Naming it gave me access to what the abuse really was. When I first said out loud to other people that I had been sexually abused by a member of my family, I had no idea what I was getting myself into. All I knew was that I needed to tell the truth. It felt like the first time in my life I had ever told the truth to anyone.

Only by saying the words *incest* and *sexual abuse* was I able to begin to discover the extent of the damage that abuse did. It was also the first step in accessing other incest memories. After processing the first several memories of incest, my psyche, my system, was more able and better prepared for the deeper truths about my childhood.

It was a year and a half later when I had my first memory of ritual abuse. As I see it now, that period was one during which I was subconsciously preparing myself to receive the shock that would follow. I was building a new relationship with myself based on new information that altered my perception of the world.

During this year and a half, I was learning the emotional vocabulary I needed to communicate with my subconscious, my inner children, my soul. These inner kids had been talking to me for years, but in languages I couldn't understand—body memories, flashbacks, nightmares, night terrors, addictions, self-abuse, depression, and so on. I devoted myself to becoming fluent in these heart languages.

Only then did the deeper, long lost memories of satanic ritual abuse come. I did not know they were coming. I just knew that for the first time I was trusting my own inner instinct no matter what.

Before that time, I wasn't strong enough to face the pain of what I had experienced. It would have been too much; it would somehow have broken me. In a way it did.

Programming

 I have seen a lot of killing and hurting of people—mostly children. I have also taken part in that hurting. My participation was forced, but that can never change the fact that I was there and that I did do those things.

Participate or we will hurt you or members of your family. Don't tell or we will hurt the ones you love. Above all, remember that it never really happened to begin with, and if you ever think it did, you're making it up. No one will believe you. They will think you're crazy. They'll lock you up. You will kill yourself. Mary had a little lamb. They'll lock you up. They'll kill your sister. Mary had a little lamb. No one will believe you. It can't be true. It can't be true. Its fleece was white as snow.

I was often raped or forced to hurt others, but I never really felt it. I saw it. I didn't like it. I threw up and sometimes cried (quietly). But mostly I shut down and instinct took over. A lot of people who are forced into this stuff become persons with multiple personalities. I don't know why I didn't. Sometimes I wish I had. I did come pretty close though, I know that. I have a certain connection and understanding with all of the multiples I've met along the way.

Some nights when I shut my eyes, all I see is the abuse. Sometimes it seems like it's finally going to snap me. And then I think that I can't really tell anyone because they'll never believe me. I spent my whole life trying to believe there had to be another explanation for the way I am. I would have accepted any other explanation in the world but this one. And then I feel like if someone does believe me, they will think I am so gross and defective that they'll never talk to me again. Or it would turn out they were in the cult all along, just waiting for me to slip up and talk.

One of the things that has been the hardest for me to get a handle on is the programming. At the same time, learning about the programming validated my experience more than just about anything. My entire adulthood has been plagued and haunted with extreme and violent episodes of self-hatred. This all began to come out for me after I got sober from drugs and alcohol. Even though I still used compulsive sex to medicate my feelings, I could not produce the state of incapacitated oblivion that adequately repressed this programming.

So as an adult, some seemingly small, insignificant event would trigger an episode of shame and self-hatred. If I didn't actually bang my head against the wall, I fantasized about it. I would almost certainly punch the wall, throw something that would smash against the wall, and break furniture or lamps. I would scream, "F—— you, God. F—— Jesus. I hate you. You've ruined my life." This would escalate until I was exhausted or lost my voice. I would tell my friends in recovery that I had been doing "anger work."

It took eight years of these episodes before I understood with any degree of confidence and certainty that I was reacting to the programming of the cult as a result of being triggered in the here and now.

I finally reached the place where I began to talk about these episodes, to allow them to come and not resist them, to be taught by them. Most importantly, I was able to identify the triggers so that I could learn to manage the programming better, find the source, and diffuse the feelings.

A Long Way to Healing

Some experts say that recovery from satanic ritual abuse takes eight or ten years before you can fully integrate your hurt and history into a holistic perspective. I don't know. I know I see some years ahead of this. I have been in this period of recovery for a year now.

I have been deeply hurt. I still become confused pretty easily, and sometimes I get disoriented. I dissociate a lot (less than I used to), whenever I need to be safe. I still test people's trust over and over. I am extremely protective of my privacy and my space. I have posttraumatic stress disorder and maybe an atypical dissociative disorder. Whatever.

But I have come a long, long way. And I have survived. I am alive, for one thing. I am not autistic, emotionally handicapped, learning disabled, electively mute, mentally retarded, as many victims of satanic abuse are diagnosed (and may legitimately become as a result of their trauma). I am not an actively practicing alcoholic, a prostitute, a child molester, or a violent criminal, as many victims are. Remarkably, I am neither spending my life in jail or in a mental institution, as many other victims of satanic abuse do. Finally, I have not been misdiagnosed as borderline, schizophrenic, manic-depressive, schizophrenoform, or delusional, and medicated into oblivion, as many survivors are.

Instead, I am here to tell you the truth so that we as a society can begin to prevent this culture of killing.

I need people in my life who know my truth and are willing to risk being a part of my life anyway. I need friends who are willing to watch me grow, stumble, and grow some more. I need people who are patient and tolerant, yet who are safely confrontive and responsible, and who expect the same from me. I need people who understand that this is a very slow process that cannot, under any circumstances, be rushed or forced.

I am committed to breaking the silence that has held me captive for thirty years. Though I am afraid of abandonment, ridicule, and repercussions, I will not be silent. The silence is killing me.

I am just one. Together, we are many. We are hurt, but we are alive. We are making it. Life has meaning for us, and god cares very deeply for each of us. Though the general public may not see the value of advocating for us now, they soon will. They will understand that we, all of us, are threatened by satanic crime.

I know today that god loves me very much and wants me to be comfortable in this life. God did not bring me this far to drop me. God is doing everything for me that I could not do for myself. And god has given me the courage to reach out and to speak out with this story.

I would not ever venture to write these things down if I did not care for you very much. I write from a caring I have for myself. Writing my story may seem like an odd way to care about someone, but it seems that if I am to be able to walk free in this world, my story must be told.

I am learning now how to be in my body, how to accept who I am and where I'm at. Much is still tentative in my life. As I reclaim myself and regain my power, I am more fully aware of the richness of life and the wholeness god is teaching me. It is slowly coming.

CHAPTER FIVE

Reprogramming:
Overcoming Mind Control

Souls are made of endurance.
—Carl Sandburg (unpublished piece from a notebook of 1902)

What Is Programming?

As we remember and heal from the abuse, we discover internal messages that we received as a part of the abuse. These messages are referred to as *programming*. They are messages about our life, our values, our personhood, our purpose in being. They are messages that, when examined in light of reality, are false and detrimental to our reclaiming wholeness.

 Programming has been described as feeling like there is a big magnet pulling one toward destruction. When everything except hurting or killing oneself seems illogical and hopeless, programming is very likely at work.

Many who grow up in less-than-functional families discover internal messages such as "I am no good," "I can't do anything right," "I can't make it." These messages are often called *shame messages*. They reflect the shame that we carry from our experience of growing up but that we no longer need to hold in our lives of recovery. It is important to identify and let go of these shame messages that we inherited from our families.

Programming messages are similar to shame messages in that they are false and they hinder our recovery. They are different from shame messages because programming was intentionally given to us as a part of our abuse. In this context programming is mind control.

USE OF MIND CONTROL IN ABUSE SETTINGS

Abusers incorporate programming and mind control into ritual abuse to ensure such things as secrecy, submission, behavioral molding, indoctrination, long-term control, and shaping of future participation in the cult or organization.

The programming messages as well as the experience of receiving them are repressed with the memories of the abuse. Hidden in the subconscious, they act as subliminal messages shaping the lives of those who carry them. During the process of healing from ritual abuse, programming messages are uncovered and are corrected so that they no longer negatively influence the life of the survivor.

Sometimes the recollection of a programming message is accompanied by the memory of the situation in which the message was given. In cases of satanic abuse, programming may take place within a ritual and given as a verbal command or a chant which is repeated during the abuse. Some forms of abuse are for the express purpose of instilling programming messages. Electric shock to different parts of the body, prolonged periods of isolation, sexual abuse or beatings, and other types of painful torture may be accompanied by spoken messages or coerced behavior to pattern programming messages into the minds of victims.

Examples of Programming Messages

Programming messages may be difficult to recognize at first. They have been a part of us for a long time, buried with the memories of abuse. They manifest themselves in subtle ways, through feelings and behaviors, rather than through billboardlike thoughts. But as we work to recover from our abuse and the false beliefs we carry, we are able to recognize when programming is at work, and the messages become clear. Some programming messages that other survivors have identified are listed in the following sections.

CAUTION TO THE READER

It is important for you to use caution in reading programming messages because they may trigger your own programming. Please skip to page 84 if you are not in a safe space to read these messages. Or use your support network or helpers to help you decide when to read the rest of this chapter. Don't forget to ask for help if you need it.

PROGRAMMING FOR SECRECY

These messages encourage victims to keep the abuse a secret:

> If you tell, you will go to hell.
> Don't tell, or I'll kill you.
> Never tell. If you tell, someone will die.
> Don't tell, because this is private. If you tell, you will not be a part of your family any more.
> No one will ever believe you. They will think you are crazy.

PROGRAMMING FOR SUBMISSION AND CONTROL

These programming messages enforce the survivor's behavior, keeping him or her in the control of the abusers. They keep the victim in a place of helplessness and dependency:

> You can never get away.
> You will never survive without us.
> Do what I say, or I will kill your brother (or your sister, etc.).
> If anyone finds out what you did, you will be locked up.
> You will always be one of us.

PROGRAMMING FOR INDOCTRINATION

Indoctrination messages work to shape the victim's beliefs and values to match those of the cult. Programming of this type may be a part of the initiation and training process that ensures the victim a place in the group:

> Jesus/God is bad.
> You belong to Satan.
> Black people/Catholics/homosexuals/etc. are bad and should die.
> You are evil. You are filled with evil.
> You are married to Satan.
> Jesus/God hates you and will never accept you.
> Killing/blood gives you life.
> Satan is God.

PROGRAMMING FOR FUTURE PARTICIPATION AND CONTROL

Some programming has the effect of insuring future participation in cult activity or future control by the cult. This type of programming includes messages that instruct the victim to come back to the cult of origin at a certain age or circumstance (when one gets married, has children, etc.). Other messages instruct the person or one of the alters to perform a specified task on a particular ritual date. Some programming gives instructions for self-destruction in case programming to return to the cult does not work. These messages attempt to cause the survivor to hurt or kill him/herself.

Healing from Programming

The process of healing from programming involves recognizing the programming and replacing it with new, positive messages. Healing from programming is a slow and difficult process. Programming is hard to see because it is so close to us and so much a part of us. As we move through healing, we become better able to identify when we are overcome with programming and better able to live into messages of health and truth.

RECOGNIZING PROGRAMMING

Survivors can recognize the presence of programming in several ways. If a person is participating in behavior that is harmful or detrimental to the health of the whole, there may be self-destructive programming involved. For example, self-harming behavior such as self-mutilation, addictions, or suicidal ideation may be fueled by programming.

Irrational thinking or judgment about self may indicate programming messages. Thoughts that the survivor is worthless and should die indicate these messages.

Inability to share about abuse in a usually safe setting may be caused by programming messages about secrecy.

Often survivors need assistance to begin to recognize programming. Once you begin to learn to recognize it, then it is easier to find. You may want to ask a friend to help you by giving you feedback if they recognize that your thinking is irrational or statements you are making are false.

1. When you find yourself thinking irrationally, write the statements down on a piece of paper. Next to the irrational thought or statement, write down any the message or assumption that underlies it. For example, *irrational thought:* If I see a policeman, I will be arrested; *underlying message:* The police will get me.
2. Once you have identified the message or assumption, ask yourself whether it is true or false today.
3. If the statement or thought is false, test whether the message is programming. Ask yourself, "Where or when did I learn this message? Who gave it to me? Is this a message that came from my abuse? Where or when in my abuse? Can I identify the time when I received this message? What was the purpose of the message?"
4. If you are having trouble answering the questions, ask whether anyone inside knows the answers to any of the questions.

It may be helpful to examine your experiences of abuse to see what messages were forced upon you as a part of the abuse. As you process a memory of abuse, ask yourself, "What message did I learn from this experience? Is this a belief or statement that I still carry today? Is this a message that I want to include as a part of my life now?"

CREATING NEW MESSAGES

As you are able to identify programming messages that you carry, you can begin to let go of the harmful programming and replace it with new, healthy messages.

It may be helpful to write down the steps of the process. first, identify the programming message. Second, write *true* or *false* next to the message. Third, if the message is false, write next to it the message that you would prefer to carry with you.

For example, the message that you identify is, "I will never get away unless I die." The message is false because the abuse is not happening today. The new message for today is, "Today I am safe and can protect all of me. I don't have to get away any more. I have gotten safely away, and I did not die."

It may be helpful for you to write and talk about your learnings. Write about your process in your journal. Talk in your therapy session or in support groups about the programming you have discovered. As you process your learnings, the power of the mind control is taken away. As you share with others, you build a network of people who can help you remember your reality during times when you are confused or having difficulty.

Every time you sense the message given to you in the abuse, repeat the truth and remind yourself of your new reality. Countering the old messages with the new enables you to create a healthier, more accurate reality for yourself. This is the way that you heal from the programming.

Use this exercise by Caryn StarDancer to help you work through and process programming messages.

Reprogramming Worksheet[1]

by Caryn StarDancer

Trigger:

Immediate Response:
    Emotion:
    Message:

Short-Term Consequences:
    Emotion:
    Message:

Challenge:
    Old message:
    Is this message based on fact?
    What facts refute this message?
    What facts, if any, support it?

Results:
    What is the worst that could happen?
    What favorable things, if any, might happen?

New Program:
    What alternative thought could I try to replace the old
        message with?
    How might I defuse my negative emotions?
    What things can I do to replace them with positive
        emotions?

HONORING SURVIVAL

As you work with uncovering mind control messages and replacing them, you will probably encounter the parts of you that received and carried those messages in the abuse. These alters/kids may be resistant to giving up the old messages. That resistance is to be expected. After all, adhering to the messages kept them safe for a long time. They may fear that giving up the old reality, breaking the injunctions imposed by the messages will cause harm or death to them.

As the one who is healing and taking care of all the parts within, you will be the one working with these resistant parts of you. Tell them that they are safe today and that you will protect them. Honor their courage and their role in keeping you alive. They deserve great praise for the jobs that they did very well.

You can assure them that you are grateful for their jobs well done. And you can let them know that you are working for their best interest as you let go of the secrets and messages that they carry. They will not be harmed, because you are living a new way today. In fact, the messages given them were false. They were lies that were told to them by the people that hurt them. Gently tell them what the truth is today.

Sometimes, parts of you have been programmed with a particular job assignment. When you uncover alters who have been programmed to harm someone, ask for help from your therapist or helper. The primary task is to ensure your safety and the safety of all of your kids. Together, you and your therapist can work with the alter to find out specifically what the job is, when it is to be done, who told them to it, and what will happen if they do not do it. In addition, work with the alter to help him or her know the truth today: that he or she does not have to complete the job because the abuse is over; that he or she is safe today; that no one will suffer consequences from the abusers for not doing his or her job. It may be helpful to work with that inner child to find a new job that is not harmful and will benefit the system. (See the section titled "Creative Problem Solving" in chapter 4.)

As you work with all of the parts of you, you are shedding programming messages and creating a reality for today. The task of reprogramming is the same whether it is for you or for any of the parts within you. You are reshaping and reframing your thoughts, your feelings, your behaviors. You are healing the wounds of the trauma. You are setting yourself free.

CHAPTER SIX

Loss and Grief

"Crazy" feelings are a normal part of the grief process. . . . Having "crazy" feelings does not mean that you are crazy. It just means that you are normal.

—Paul Kent Froman, *After You Say Goodbye*

EXQUISITE PAIN
(For the nephew I may never know.)

Welcome to the world, Matthew Bryan.
I am your aunt.
I am so very happy that you have come
into the world.

All of my being asks
to see you, to meet you,
to hold you.

But the cruel chains that
bound my youth
bind you now,
keep me from you.

Forgive me, Matthew Bryan.
I do not mean to punish you
for the sins
of the past.

I would give almost
anything
to be a part of your life.

But the Almost
is more than I can give.

I give you my love,
my prayers,
my hope,
and I think of you growing
into a little boy.

Perhaps
someday
we
will
meet.

Aunt Emilie

Feeling the Pain of Loss

We ritual abuse survivors know loss that few others today have known. Loss is our constant companion even as we gain back a life we may never have had.

The irony of the exquisite pain of loss is that we do not receive new life unless we feel the pain of our losses. Sometimes we feel as though we have lost everything: our past, our family (parents, siblings, grandparents, aunts and uncles, nephews and nieces), our childhood, our abilities to relate to human beings, our health, our wealth, our children.

What is difficult to see and feel during the times we are grieving loss is that grieving and letting go are the only ways to open our wounded selves to the new growth of health and life within us.

That aching emptiness is the home of new community, deeper connectedness with a higher power, new meaning for life.

We will open this chapter about loss and grief by looking at the grief process for ritual abuse survivors. Then we will look at some of the types of loss that ritual abuse survivors experience and hear stories of survivors' experiences of loss and grief. Finally, we will examine some ways of grieving and letting go of losses.

About Grief

Grief is what we feel when we have lost someone or something. It is a normal part of life and a necessary part of healing. Grief is the process that allows us to move through losses and into life again. It is "a complex of several different emotions, one of which is sadness. The others are usually anger, guilt, and fear. Any unpleasant emotion (such as frustration, bitterness, or resentment) can be part of the grieving process, as we struggle to come to grips with our loss."[1]

Grieving takes a long time. It is a cyclical process. The grief process moves on over time, ever deeper into the heart of pain and the freedom of letting go. You may feel that you have grieved a loss only to find that it surfaces again many months later. You did nothing wrong. You are in the *process* of grieving. Over time, the process brings us back to a loss to grieve it on a different, deeper level. This cycle of feeling the loss, having space from the feelings, and feeling the loss in a new way continues for a long time. The pain lessens over time, although it may not ever completely go away.

The process of grief for ritual abuse survivors is much more intense than for "normal" people. Children normally will experience losses of pets, of grandparents; sometimes they will know the loss of parents, siblings, or friends. Older people experience deaths of family members and friends more frequently. But most people do not experience in their lives the kinds or numbers of losses that ritual abuse survivors know. To see losses on the same or greater magnitude, we must look at the experiences of people in wartime or in today's AIDS epidemic.

One person who has studied grief from the perspective of catastrophic loss is Dr. Paul Kent Froman. He has worked with many persons with HIV/AIDS and their families and friends. Froman has found that the traditional idea of "stages of grief"[2] is not helpful for people dealing with such huge losses. "It is too simplistic to be relevant to AIDS deaths, partly because there are so many of them. The stages of grieving over one death soon bang up against the stages of another one, and another one, and so on. The result is a chaos of emotion."[3]

It is important to realize that ritual abuse survivors, too, experience loss at such levels that working through "stages" of grief may not be helpful. We survivors experience a new loss every time we discover another abuser in our past; every time we remember another category of abuse that we experienced; every time we have to set a boundary with a family member. These losses upon losses make it impossible to move through grief in a logical, organized way. About the time one has begun to feel anger at one's grandfather, a memory surfaces about abuse by another family member, and we are plunged again into denial. We experience layers upon layers of grief, "a chaos of emotion."

Froman describes four "elements" of grieving: "1. Be willing to experience your feelings, as opposed to repressing or stuffing them, or getting stuck in them. 2. Realize that you are still in control of your life. 3. Grieve in your own way. 4. Be willing to take action."[4]

These elements are both simple and comprehensive. They remind us that whatever we feel is part of the process of healing; that we are in charge of our life today, and we know what we need; that we have the inner wisdom to know how to heal; and that action is a crucial part of the process. Taking action assists us in exercising the power we have today to be survivors rather than victims.

If we are experiencing overwhelming feelings, we can remember that these feelings make sense—they are normal because of what happened to us. We can realize that we are still in charge, even if we don't feel that way. We can ask ourselves what we need in order to take care of ourselves right now. And we can take action: make a phone call, wrap up in a warm blanket, be with a friend, cry, write a poem. When we feel grief, we are in the process of healing and moving toward wholeness.

Types of Losses

As ritual abuse survivors, we experience many types of losses. As we continue to make progress in our healing, we will discover losses and begin the process of grieving them. Some of the types of losses we may find are described in the paragraphs that follow.

THE LOSS OF FAMILY

We may lose some or all of our family of origin because they are not safe. We may suspect or know that family members are still involved in abuse. Family members may not believe us or may invalidate our reality. They may label us as troublemakers, crazy, weak, vindictive, impressionable.

When we were children, the effects of the abuse were devastating to us. The abuse devastates our adult life as our connections with immediate and extended family are torn apart. We are separated emotionally, if not physically, from those who perpetrated our abuse or those who did not keep us safe. The abuse rips apart our relationships with siblings who may still be in contact with the abusers or who are in so much denial that contact with them would endanger our stability.

We are faced with questions: "What boundaries create safety for me and my inner children? What do I expect from those family members with whom I am in contact? If I am losing most or all of my family, what other support communities do I have? What kind of support networks do I need?"

Even as we develop families of choice for ourselves, we realize with sadness that nothing can take the place of the people we have lost. Nothing can replace the nurturing parent, the protecting grandparent, the loyal sibling we should have had. Nothing can take the place of the memories lost.

THE RIFT
(to my family)

I stand on the edge
　　and watch as you drift away.
Shifting plates create
　　　　EARTHQUAKES
that rock me.
　　　　　　You stand and see.
We are stone faced,
　　　　　　　you and I.
Fathoms of empty darkness
　　　　　　　　separate us.
I can't reach you.
　　　　　　　　　You can't hear me.

Tears slide down
　　　　　　　　　　the jagged edge
of each cliff.

THE LOSS OF PARTS OF OURSELVES

Many of our losses are within our selves. We lose parts of us, our spirituality or relationship to God, our trust of the world or other people, our health, our time and resources. We grieve for the parts of us that were scarred or permanently altered by the abuse.

Some of our losses can be repaired or replaced. We can learn skills of healthy relationships, communication, self-care. We can rebuild our selves into positive, creative, productive contributors to life. But other losses are permanent. We can never create who we would have been if we had not been abused. We cannot replace the time that we have spent to heal. We cannot erase the pain we have felt or the scars—physical, emotional, psychological, or spiritual—that we bear. And we cannot bring back the parts of us that could not survive the trauma of the abuse.

Sometimes we discover that parts of us have died as a result of the abuse. As we get to know our inner children, we may find that some did not survive the abuse. We grieve for the parts of us that we will not be able to reclaim, because they were destroyed.

Healing from these losses, we sift through our lives as though they were burned-out houses. We look through the ashes for parts of us that survived the flames, for keepsakes that can be mended. We assess the parts of us that must be rebuilt to bring us to wholeness. We can build new realities, new selves, new lives. But we cannot replace what was lost.

Tracy's Loss

I had sensed for a long time that I had lost a part of myself. After a particularly tragic memory, I experienced the presence of a deeply wounded young child. Since she was unable to sustain life on her own, I placed her into a healing cocoon of light in my safe place. She remained there. I sat by her, holding her, stroking her cheek, trying to will life back into her. But it was not meant to be. The damage was too great.

She remained in the light like she was lying in state while I grieved. She touched a level of grief deeper than I had ever experienced. Then it was time to say goodbye. With the support of my therapist and fellow survivors, I let her go. I retained her energy, but I released her spirit to the universe. The clouds are now her playground.

I still miss her terribly. I believe, though, that someday with my own passing we will reconnect in our wholeness.

I cannot logically tell you what happened. I simply know that she was a part of me and that now she is gone. Perhaps she was not able to escape after the abuse and became stuck in a deep, dark place within me. Reliving the memory somehow freed her. Was she a part of me that died? I think so.

THE LOSS OF CHILDREN TO THE ABUSE

 Memories of ritual abuse may bring us overwhelming memories about children who were tortured or killed as a part of the abuse. These experiences of death and destruction are particularly traumatic to remember. They are experiences that no child (no human) should ever have to go through.

In some cases, we saw other children killed while we were left alive. Each of us knows that he or she could have been the one killed. Our grief brings with it a mixture of sadness and terror. It also brings with it "survivor guilt"—questions about why we lived and others did not.

For those of us who are female, we may have had the particular horror of having seen our own newborn child, fetus, or older child taken from us and destroyed. This loss is excruciating. It is unbearable to have lost that child, that intimate relationship of mother and child.

"A child who dies becomes the center of the universe: stars and meadows die with him."[5]

Anna's Child

 I will never forget the moment when I remembered losing a child to the cult. It washed over me in a sickening wave of realization. When I was fourteen, I was pregnant. They aborted the fetus and destroyed it in a ritual. I was forced to participate. As I went through the flashback, the alter who experienced this event was coming apart with grief. She wanted to go with the baby to death. When I came back from the flashback, I too felt overwhelming grief. I also felt something strange—a feeling of emptiness. I am childless, but I have carried life within me. I had a *baby* growing inside of me, a life which was taken from me. I realized that the child would be twenty years old, had she lived. I would have been a good mother, loving my child and protecting her from any harm.

I felt the pain of grief for a long time. I still feel sad when I think of the child that I lost. I feel especially sad since I am childless now. Part of my grieving process led me to write a message to the child I lost. Writing, creating something that expresses my feelings, honors her and assures me that she will not be forgotten.

I never had a chance to be a mom.
They took you from me
Before I even knew you were there.
They said I was dead inside,
That they were taking my life force from me.

And they did. They took you.
You were so small you almost weren't anything.
They destroyed you—flesh of my flesh, blood of my blood.

I'm sorry, little one. If I'd had the chance,
I would have loved and cared for you.
If I could, I would
Wrap you in a soft, warm blanket
And rock you till you go to sleep.
I would give you a furry bunny to cuddle close
And protect you from any evil ones.

You would be safe and protected and cherished,
A precious child of your higher power's,
A precious child of mine . . .
But I never had the chance to be your mom.

THE LOSS OF WHO WE ARE (WHO WE THOUGHT WE WERE)

We were able to stay alive by repressing our childhood abuse. That means that as we remember and accept the truth of our past, we lose the childhood we remembered prior to the abuse. We lose the fantasy of the childhood we never had, the childhood where we were loved, taken care of, and protected by our families. We lose the families and communities that are an integral part of our personhood.

Sometimes the memories of abuse shatter our view of our own self, our innocence, our integrity, our morality. Ritual abuse often includes situations where victims are forced to become perpetrators. You may come to realize that you were forced to hurt a child, a baby, an animal. You may have even been forced to participate in the death of another person.

Words cannot ease the devastation of this realization.

Survivors feel disbelief, numbness, terror, sadness, and tremendous guilt. It is as if someone has taken away our own life story and replaced it with another. This loss of who we thought we were must be grieved, too, for survivors to recover life.

Remembering these losses is very difficult and can send survivors into feelings of despair. It is crucial to use the support that you have when you are feeling overwhelmed. Remember that you are not at fault for your abuse or any elements of it. The perpetrators are *always* the ones responsible for what happens in situations of abuse. (See the section "Feeling Evil" in chapter 7.)

As you are able, sort out the pieces that need to be grieved and let yourself feel the feelings. You are not alone. Your feelings are normal. Today you are in control of your life. You have within you what you need to heal. You can take the actions that are needed.

The loss of who we thought we were brings us to question who we really are, who the people in our childhood really were. We are left to ask such questions as: "What does it mean for me today that so much of my history has been shattered? Who am I today? How do the things that I experienced affect who I am today? What are the things I value about me? What things do I need to let go of from my past? from my abuse?"

Grieving Losses

1. Make a list of your specific losses. You will probably not be able to remember them all at one time. Begin to write down your losses and add to the list as you are able to remember them. Put a dot (●) beside the losses you have begun to grieve. Put a square (□) beside the losses you are ready to begin letting go. Put a check (✓) beside the losses you have already let go.
2. Ask yourself, "What were the feelings I felt as I listed my losses? Did I feel sad? Did I feel numb?"
3. Look at your list and choose one or two losses that you would like to explore more deeply. Take some time to write about that loss. Describe it. Remember stories, experiences, images, sensations. Write down your reflections and your feelings.
4. If you are experiencing feelings, stop and let yourself feel them.
5. If you are feeling numb or if you need to postpone your feelings to another time, take time to consider these questions: "What are some ways I can allow myself to explore and experience my grief? When will I make time to feel these feelings?"
6. Make a plan to regularly check in with your grief, to listen for times when you need to be able to express feelings, and to feel the feelings rather than stuffing them. Share your plan with a friend or helper and then follow through with it.

WAYS TO EXPRESS GRIEF

Lots of us believe we don't know how to grieve. We never learned how to listen to and feel our emotions. Grief does not have to result in an hour-long cry, although it may. We can process and express grief in numerous ways. Sometimes expressing grief will consist of remembering something and feeling sad and heavy for a few minutes. Other times, grief will fill us with many tears, shed over several days.

Following are some ways that grief may be expressed. Think of times when you have experienced grief and add your own ideas.

Ways to Express Grief

Cry.
Draw or paint a picture.
Write a letter, poem, story, or song.
Rock your bear.
Sing or play music.
Talk to a friend or helper.
Write your own ideas in your journal.

SYMBOLIZING LOSSES AND LETTING GO

Eventually, grieving brings us to a point where we become ready to let go of a loss. This letting go often happens little bits at a time. We may never be able to let go completely. But we will reach the point where the grief does not debilitate our lives. We will be able to hold the loss more in a gentle cradle of sadness than in a vise grip of despair or anger.

As you work with your losses, reflect on ways you can symbolize your grief and the letting go of losses. Before letting go of a loss, ask yourself whether everyone on the inside has had a chance to say or feel whatever they need to express. Do you sense that all of you is ready to let go of a loss, or is there more grieving to be done?

If you have the sense that it is time to let go, consider using an action that symbolizes the letting go. Symbolizing the loss is a healthy way to ritualize the letting go and the freedom toward which you are moving. Think of ways you can symbolize specific losses and letting go. Here are some suggestions:

Write a letter to say goodbye.
Paint pictures that show the loss and letting go.
Create something new at the place of the loss.
Make a divorce certificate.
Create a liturgy or service of letting go.
Do a guided imagery picturing yourself letting go.
Write your own ideas in your journal.

Hope in the Midst of Grief

Is there a message of hope about grief and loss? There is no way to make sense of the losses we experienced or replace what we lost. It is, in fact, senseless that we were victims of ritual abuse and that we lost so much. It is not right. But many things in life are not right and do not make sense. If we can glean hope or meaning from all we have been through, it may be that we survived and that we are strong, creative, wonderful people despite what they tried to create in us. The hope may be that we have escaped the cycle of violence and that we can pass on to the next generation a legacy of gentleness and compassion.

As you go through the process of grieving and healing from your losses, remember: Grieving takes time. Grieving involves pain. Tears are essential. Pain will not last forever. You will feel better. Grief is a part of healing. You are not alone.

Living the Questions

Tracy is a survivor of satanic ritual abuse who is learning to re-claim and rebuild life "on the side of the good." She is a profes-sional, a writer, a mother seeking to provide a safe and meaning-ful life for her children. She shares with us some of her questions and reflections about living with the legacy of ritual abuse and breaking free from its wounds.

I

I don't believe it is possible to be a survivor of ritual abuse without undergoing a deep, spiritual crisis. I still feel deeply mired in mine, struggling to fit my childhood reality into a spiritual framework. Perhaps some find it easier to ignore the spiritual realm. However, the quintessential question for me is how to fight Evil.[1] How not to be "one of them." How to live on the side of Good. To do these things requires grappling with my spiritual beliefs.

My realization that I was a ritual survivor profoundly affected me. In some ways it totally shattered my old ideas about god. Who was this loving god I had heard about all my life? How could god be loving if god would not save those children I saw sacrificed? How could god be all-powerful, all-protecting, omnipotent? Ob-viously god could be none of these and also be good. Good gods didn't watch the massacre of innocents when they had it within their power to act. Good gods did something. How could I place the heinous reality of ritual abuse into a spiritual framework while still embracing the god I knew?

The answer was that I could not. Instead, I railed at this god. I hated this god—"the bastard god," as my friend said. Finally, in the midst of the deepest spiritual crisis of my life, I renounced this god.

Thus began a period in my recovery marked by confusion and imbalance. Having rejected the bastard god, what was left? Was there anything? I felt empty—alone. I could not and would not pray. I had lost my sense of anchoring.

I struggled with my beliefs as I read several books that addressed Good and Evil and the battle between them. One author had the guts to say that god was not an all-powerful, all-protecting god, since god did not miraculously pluck children from harm's path.[2]

Another author talked about spiritual crises.[3] She described a process of waiting and listening in the midst of the crisis. Further, she talked about living the question. I knew then that although I did not have my answer, I had my process. I waited. I simply waited, but I waited actively, immersing myself in the questions.

Ritual survivors have many questions. There are questions about who god is and who satan is. There is the question about what drives humanity to choose Evil. There are also those more personal and tedious questions that plague survivors: "Did I make it up? Is it really true? Am I crazy?"

In the past I ran from the panic incipient in those questions. However, living the questions required that I struggle with my panic. So I waited. And struggled. Even though facing that panic was uncomfortable, I found it to be a profound process, moving me toward new insights and new questions but answers as well.

During this period of active waiting, certain truths became apparent. I had to create a completely different vision of god. Today I think of God/Good as a light energy, an energy of creation that flows within and without so that it is a part of me, as I am a part of it.

But the process, rather than the exact belief, is what I wish to convey. When I trust nothing else, I trust my process, for I know it works. It leads me in due time to what I need. Even though a part of me still aggressively attacks each new task of recovery, my process is now complemented by a stance of waiting—an active waiting as I live the question. I live the question. I embrace it. I challenge it. And ultimately I grow from it.

II

Although I am learning to wait, I am basically a person of action. I must do. As I progressed in my recovery and became more aware of the barbarity of the abuse, I was filled with an outrage that demanded voice. But how could I vent my outrage? It was not yet time for me to make public my private hell. I felt impotent and shackled.

So I wrote. At first I wrote in secret, silenced by my shame at expressing myself. Later I shared some of my writings with my therapist. Long after that, I shared some writings with a friend. And another . . . then another.

I also began to write professionally. I had to. The outrage inside demanded a voice. Because I would not go public, I had to use the voice of others. So I researched the work of experts in the fields of sexual and ritual abuse. Then I wrote the truth as I know it. I quoted fact after fact, finding after finding, and so voiced the outrage of my abused child and my wounded adult.

Even as I wrote, though, I knew deep inside that I was healing—by venting. By saying how bad it really was.

THE FIRE WITHIN

The words flow,
falling over themselves in a flood to get out,
to be put down on paper so that others will know—
so that they will finally and totally know—
how bad it really was.

Listen to me, I say,
and if you will not hear me,
then hear those who study,
those who project,
those who analyze
what they do not really know.

Not as I know;
not as I have lived,
have experienced,
have breathed it.

For I own the truth.
It is mine and it is I.
It is the who I am,
the child who was invaded countless times.

Yes, I know the effects.
I am the effects.
I am also the struggle to heal.

I am the voice who knows.
Hear what I have to say.

III

My children were four and six when I had my first ritual memory.
They were the perfect ages to enjoy Halloween. The older child
had by this time enough recall to be caught up in the excitement of
the preparation. She had listed every person's house she wanted to
visit, including those of distant relatives. My younger child for the
first time understood what Halloween was about. This understanding brought such childish delight that it radiated in her eyes and in
her step. This should have been a special time for us. But Halloween would not be the same for me again.

That year I felt assaulted by the continual parade of witches, warlocks, and childish demons that paraded by our house. I knew what was really happening. In the early evening, children run door to door. Later, though, in the deep of the night, children would be desecrated on altars as sacrifices. Children would die.

I hurt deeply that first Halloween. I grieved and mourned. As a parent I mourned, knowing that I could never again fully enjoy my children's innocence at Halloween. I also mourned the brutal abuse of the me within who suffered at the hands of Evil. And I mourned the loss of life to come.

That first year, I spent Halloween evening with my support group. At that time I knew no other ritual survivors. My support group heard my grief and pain and mourned with me. That night I also robbed them of some of their innocence about Halloween, because now they also knew. Could they ever undo that knowledge? I knew that I could not.

HALLOWEEN

Ghosts, goblins, children in the night
running house to house gathering loot,
tripping over shoes too big, gowns too long,
awash in laughter,
in the free spirit of the child.
Oh, to relish those days again.

Tonight, though, I mourn
for the child in me,
for the children who tonight will be slaughtered
as lambs are, in sacrifice.
I pray for their spirits
even as I rail at the god who will not protect them.

May they be taken quickly.
May they escape the atrocities.
May they be spared drinking the blood,
eating the flesh of a spirit newly gone.

May this world stop for a moment in time
and acknowledge their deaths.
But it will not.

So tonight, in memoriam,
I grieve your death, your mutilation.
Child, I pray for the life you never lived.

God, take these children.
Ease their tortured passing.
Bring them close to you.
Hold them.
Love them.

But for those children
who are not so lucky to die,
for those survivors who
in witnessing the torture
lost portions of themselves,
God, help them
as they must live in their agony.

God, help them.
Hold them.
Love them.

And, God, help me.

After that first year it became important for me to reclaim Halloween in some way. My children deserved, and I wanted my children
to have, innocent memories of their Halloweens. As I could, I began accompanying them as they "looted" the neighborhood. I also
needed to establish my own ritual of healing and remembering.
That ritual is evolving. Within it I honor my child and the agony
she endured, I acknowledge those who will lose their lives, and I
acknowledge those who will survive in their agony. It is about fighting back. This healing ritual is my outrage, and it is my voice.

CHAPTER SEVEN

FACING EVIL

There is evil in the world; you must not let us forget this.
—Elie Wiesel and Albert H. Friedlander, *The Six Days of Destruction*

Many Questions

When we start acknowledging and dealing with our ritual abuse we are shocked not only by the fact that we were abused so horribly, but also by the realization that human beings are capable of committing such atrocities against others.

Questions come to our minds:

How could something like this happen?
How could so many people be killed and no one do anything?
Why didn't someone stop it?
Where was God when all this was going on?

These are legitimate questions. And they are questions that might never be answered adequately. The questions of why and how are the deep, yearning questions that come from a part of us that knows that nothing like ritual abuse should ever happen to anyone. They come from the part of us that knows that what happened to us is contrary to the way the world was intended to be. That part of us is outraged and saddened and sickened and horrified. Our questions come from the place within us that cries out against such evil, that life-clinging part of us that helped to keep us alive. That tiny spark of justice within us could not be put out even in the most horrible, degrading experiences a human being can go through.

It is out of the strength of that place, that spark of life, that we question how and why evil exists.

The Question of Evil

People have always struggled to explain the presence of evil in the world. Traditionally, theologians and philosophers have explored evil by looking at the nature of God and the nature of human beings.

HUMAN BEINGS

"Human beings are basically bad." "Human beings are basically good." "Human beings are basically good but can be manipulated by evil to do bad things." "Human beings are created to have choice and can choose either good or evil."

Philosophers have long argued over whether humans are by nature good or evil. What is more likely is that human beings are "by nature neither good nor evil and that both [the] good and [the] evil are human qualities and that [we have] the freedom to actualize either good or evil."[1]

Harold Kushner, in *When Bad Things Happen to Good People*, says:

> Our being human leaves us free to hurt each other, and God can't stop us without taking away the freedom that makes us human. Human beings can cheat each other, rob each other, hurt each other, and God can only look down in pity and compassion at how little we have learned over the ages about how human beings should behave.[2]

 It is painfully obvious to ritual abuse survivors that, for whatever reason, human beings are capable of and sometimes choose to do evil. This is not inconsistent with historical experience. In the Judeo-Christian tradition, the first murder was committed by one brother, Cain, against his brother, Abel. Herod, the king when Jesus was born, ordered the murder of all male children of a certain age and location. Herod wanted to kill Jesus because he was a perceived threat to Herod's throne.

Adolf Hitler and his followers were responsible for the murders of millions of people in the Holocaust during World War II. And the United States government chose to drop the atomic bomb on the civilian populations of Hiroshima and Nagasaki, Japan, during the same war.

Why do human beings torture, sacrifice, murder, and make war on each other? And how can parents submit their innocent children to the tortures of satanic rituals?

Aleksandr Solzhenitsyn said in his book *The Gulag Archipelago*:

> If only it were all so simple! If only there were evil people somewhere insidiously committing evil deeds and it were necessary only to separate them from the rest of us and destroy them. But the dividing line between good and evil cuts through the heart of every human being, and who is willing to destroy a piece of his [or her] own heart?[3]

Human beings are complicated creatures, capable of both tender love and horrible evil. How can we make sense of this paradox? And what kind of higher power created such a dilemma? These questions lead us to the other side of this exploration—the nature of God.

THE NATURE OF GOD

Yossarian, a character in Joseph Heller's novel *Catch-22*, expresses it well: "Good God, how much reverence can you have for a Supreme Being who finds it necessary to include tooth decay in [the] divine system of creation? Why in the world did [God] ever create pain?"[4]

For ritual abuse survivors, the nature and character of God is often a baffling puzzle. We were told that God did not love or care about us or God would have stopped the abuse. We were told that if God had any power, it was shadowed by the power of Satan. We were told that God ordered or supported the actions we witnessed or experienced. We were programmed, manipulated, tortured, coerced, battered, terrorized until we could believe nothing but what they said. The overwhelming evidence was that evil was the all-powerful force.

We lived lives already judged and condemned by the actions and choices our abusers forced upon us during our abuse. We had no option other than to believe and do what our abusers told us.

Today, some of us question why we are even still alive. We ask, "Is this our punishment by God? To be allowed to live and remember the horrors of our childhood? Is there even a higher power that embodies the good, the light, life? Or is it true what they told us— that Satan is the most powerful force in creation?"

If we were also taken to synagogue or church and learned traditional religious beliefs, we were often taught that God is powerful and has control over what happens in the world. If so, then why did God not stop the abuse? Does God not care about us and other victims of evil? Or is God powerless, unable, or unwilling to stop evil?

Discussions about the nature of God center around these types of questions. "Who is God? Is there a God? Does God have ultimate power over the world and human beings? Does God orchestrate events in the universe? Does God send death and destruction upon people?"

Some people believe that every death is part of God's plan. These people say that it was "God's will" that death or abuse or tragedy happened. Others believe that God does not control every human action. God gives humans choice. These people believe that because human beings have choice, they can choose actions that harm others, actions that end in death and destruction. Still others question whether God is present in people's lives, even if God is not a cosmic conductor orchestrating events in the world.

Writer and theologian Frederick Buechner writes about God's presence in the events surrounding his father's suicide:

> As I understand it, to say that God is mightily present even in such private events as these does not mean that [God] makes events happen to us which move us in certain directions like chess [pieces]. Instead, events happen under their own steam as random as rain, which means that God is present in them not as their cause but as the one who even in the hardest and most hair-raising of them offers us the possibility of that new life and healing.[5]

OTHERS QUESTION TOO

We are not alone in our confusion about the nature of human beings and the nature of God. With the Holocaust came struggles for many about the nature of God and humanity. People of all faiths wonder what events such as Auschwitz and Soweto, Treblinka and Bosnia signify about who we are as human beings and who God is to let them happen. And people come away from such evil with many different understandings and interpretations.

Theologian William Hamilton said, "God died at Auschwitz, with the death of six million Jews."[6] Jack Bemporad writes that the Holocaust has indeed demonstrated that humankind can destroy itself. It has shown that humankind "in a dehumanized state is capable of doing untold and unbelievable harm."[7]

In *The Six Days of Destruction*, a book commemorating the Holocaust, the following statement is made "to a reader rejecting prayer":

> The night was too long and too dark. The break was absolute. There are many in the Jewish tradition, in the Christian tradition, outside

all religious tradition, who have lost faith and who reject faith in
the days after the Holocaust. We can understand this, and will not
force faith. . . . And if we become too strong in our assertion that
the world is good, you must be part of our community to remind us
that the darkness is still there. There is evil in the world; you must
not let us forget this.[8]

WRESTLING WITH THE QUESTIONS

As we recover from our ritual abuse trauma, we struggle with these
and other questions and a plethora of feelings about them. It is
important to allow ourselves to ask and feel and struggle and talk
about the questions. This is a part of the process of healing from
the spiritual abuse we experienced.

Each of us makes his or her own journey through the maze of
confusion. Wherever we come out, we can be assured of these facts:
We are alive today. The abuse is not happening today. Just as we
lived through the abuse, we can live through our healing and have a
life of freedom. It is important to all of us for each of us to stay alive.

Feeling Evil

[*To the reader:* This section does not truly belong in this chapter. This is
a chapter that talks about the nature of human beings and the nature of
God, something that academics call "theology." However, survivors
have a tendency to feel responsible for everything (the rain, other
peoples' feelings, their own abuse). So it is necessary to speak to some
of the feelings that survivors may have when the topic of evil is raised.
Many times, survivors feel that they are evil in some way. But you are
not evil. Read on.]

Many survivors struggle with feeling that they are evil because
of what happened to them. However, our experiences do not make
us evil. It is important to work through these feelings, to explore

their roots, and to learn what we can from them. But it is also very important to remember that *you are not evil*. Evil things were done to and with you. But that does not make you evil.

Survivors may feel evil because of programming. Often abusers use messages such as, "You are evil, ugly, repulsive, bad, etc." to control victims. This programming ensures that the victim stays quiet. (For example: If a little girl believes she is evil or bad, she will not tell anyone what happened to her, because she will be afraid of being rejected, getting in trouble, etc.) Or the programming may be a method of coercion that forces a victim to participate in the abuser's actions. Within the setting of satanic rituals, children are told that they are possessed by evil, that they belong to Satan, etc.

It is common for ritual abuse survivors to have been forced to harm other people or animals. These forced actions are among the ways that abusers ensure their victims' continued participation. It is a method of programming that imprints in the victim the belief that he or she is one of the perpetrators, that he or she is bad and can never leave. Upon remembering these experiences, survivors feel guilt, remorse, shame, and self-hatred. While these feelings are normal responses and must be faced in order to heal, it is important to also recognize the reality: Actions taken by victims in the course of abuse are not taken in freedom. Such actions are coerced by the abusers. These actions are *always* the total responsibility of the abuser. It was *not* your fault.

Actions taken under duress are recognized universally as out of the victim's control. Military personnel go through training that prepares them for situations in which they might be hostages or prisoners. Even with this training and preparation, adults can be forced by captors to take actions against their will. Military code does not hold these persons responsible for their actions, because the actions were taken under duress. The captives were in a situation in which they had no power or choice. If these trained soldiers are not held responsible for their actions, then how can a child, a teenager, a young adult be responsible for actions they take within a situation of ritual abuse?

Use the following questions to help you process your feelings about a situation for which you feel responsible, guilty, or evil. If you feel unsafe, process the questions with your therapist or friend.

1. What was the experience that made me feel this way?
2. How old was I when it happened? How old was my abuser?
3. Who was in control?
4. Did I have a choice? If I had a choice, what was it? What would have happened if I had not taken the action?
5. What are my feelings about the experience? Are my feelings based in reality or in programming?
6. What action do I need to take to be able to let go of the feelings?

Working through these feelings is not easy. It is one of the most difficult parts of healing for ritual abuse survivors. (See Anna's story, "Baby Angels," on page 121.) It is difficult because the experiences we had are so foreign to our friends and helpers. It is difficult because of the very fact that we are human and we care. If we were truly evil, we would not care, we would not have these feelings. Do not give up. Continue to talk and write and draw and feel. You will be free.

No Answers, Just Examples

So you have not found the answers thus far in this chapter. The answer for you must be your own. Part of your healing is the process of finding the answers *for you*. Some examples follow of ways in which other abuse survivors are working this out for themselves.

Example 1: Tracy's Poem

I HATE YOU, GOD

I hate you for this world
for all the lies, the deceit
for telling us that God is love.
Well, if God is love and God is all-powerful
and if God is all-knowing,
then God is a cruel God
because God allows babies to be born
into a world to be killed—
to be slaughtered.
How is it, then, that God is good?
I hate you, God.

Example 2: Anna's Theological Understanding

I struggled much with the idea of God. The remembering of my abuse shattered my belief that there even was a God. One of my abusers was a pastor, and I felt that God was involved in my abuse through him.

My journey back to spirituality was aided when I read a book called *Of God and Pelicans*, by Jay B. McDaniel. A certain type of pelican always lays two eggs and raises only one chick. If both chicks are healthy, one of them starves to death. McDaniel questions what kind of God would allow this to happen. In an attempt to understand and develop a theology of nature, McDaniel outlines three points:

> First, we must find some way of imagining God as inexhaustibly large-hearted: that is, as so completely empathic that God is inside the skin of each sparrow, each pelican, and each sentient creature, suffering its sufferings and enjoying its joys along with it. . . .

Second, inasmuch as we deem God a creator, we must find a way of imagining God's creativity such that, even if God is responsible for the fact that there is a world as we know it, God is not indictable for worldly suffering. . . .

Third, we must find a way of articulating our hope that, while the suffering of creatures may not be preventable by God, this suffering is nevertheless redeemable by God.[9]

This Christian theology of nature has given me space for belief and hope and trust in a power greater than me. This God is not all-powerful, but is all-loving. And this God suffered with me in the midst of my abuse. This God is angry when I am angry, sad when I am sad, and holding me when I am all alone.

Example 3: Wendy Writes about the Nature of Evil

I think a lot about the nature of evil since I was exposed to so much evil growing up. I think about whether people are born evil or whether they are infected by it later in life. I think about whether there is an evil force at work in the universe or whether it is just an anomaly of nature. And I wonder why I am not infected by it in spite of all the brainwashing I underwent. These are big questions, and I don't know if I will ever know the answers. For me, the description that rings the truest came from an actor named Spalding Gray.[10] He described evil as a big dark cloud that circles the earth and settles over places like Germany, Japan, Russia, Cambodia, and the United States. Terrible things happen under this cloud, and it causes great destruction. I only hope it is lifted from my life for good.

Example 4: Mary's Beliefs

Since my memories have surfaced, I have realized the incredible horror, power, and reality of evil in this world. The evil of most people's reality is benign compared to the heinous, diabolical, and unimaginable acts that survivors of ritualistic abuse have observed and experienced. I believe that there is a real Satan, who is extremely evil and totally opposite to the true God. Satan is also very powerful. Intellectually I know that God is more powerful, but my inner kids doubt that seriously. I struggle to convince them that anyone or anything can be more powerful than those satanic evil forces.

Example 5: From a Survivor of the Holocaust

Elie Wiesel is author, teacher, 1985 recipient of the Nobel Peace Prize, and survivor of the Auschwitz concentration camp. His writings speak the questions wrung out of torture and death. He speaks eloquently through the voices of his characters. Listen to some of these voices:

Gregor argues with a rabbi: " 'After what has happened to us, how can you believe in God?' With an understanding smile on his lips the Rebbe answered, 'How can you not believe in God after what has happened?' " (From *The Gates of the Forest*.[11])

When Wiesel was fourteen years old, he witnessed the hanging of a child by the Nazis. In his novel, *Night*, the witnesses ask each other, " 'Where is God? Where is He?' someone behind me asked. . . . I heard a voice within me answer. . . : 'Where is He? Here He is—He is hanging here on this gallows.' "[12]

Raphael asks God, "Merciful God, God of Love, where were you and where was your love when under the seal of blood and fire the killers obliterated thousands of Jewish communities?" (From *Twilight*.[13])

Exploring Beliefs

The following questions are for the adult part of you to consider. You may not be able to answer them right now. These questions can be a starting place for you in considering the nature of God, human beings, and evil. Exploring one's beliefs is a lifelong process. You may find that your beliefs evolve and change over time. Explore these questions at your own pace. Write about them in your journal or talk about them with a helper or trusted friend. There are no right or wrong answers. Your answer is right because it is yours.

(Be aware that these questions may trigger programming. Write down the messages that come to your mind and consider each, one at a time. Is this message true for you today? If it is not true, what new message can you create to replace it?)

1. Is there a higher power than me? Write down its attributes.
2. Is there a name for this higher power? Does this higher power have a name for me?
3. How do I define evil? good?
4. What is my current relationship with good and evil? (Draw a picture of it.)
5. Do I believe there is an actual, personal force of evil?
6. Do I believe there is an actual, personal force of good?
7. What are my feelings about the higher power(s) I believe exist?
8. What beliefs do I yearn for in my life?
9. Talk to a trusted friend, therapist/helper, or spiritual guide about your learnings.

INTERLUDE IV

Baby Angels

Anna has been healing from her ritual abuse for three years. She works for the church, but she considers her real work to be helping others who were ritually abused. Her writing and painting have been important parts of her healing journey. Because it is quite graphic, you may want to have your therapist or a trusted friend read this story with you.

I was six years old when they dressed me in a robe, sent me to the altar, and put the ceremonial knife in my hand. I knew it was an important thing. I knew the motions to do; I had seen them many times before. My father told me that it was a doll—just a doll. I put the knife in the doll. And then I knew it was not a doll. It was a baby.

It is impossible to separate out my adult response from the response of that six-year-old. But I believe that something inside of me changed forever at that moment of realization. It was a real baby. Not a doll.

These motions became a regular part of my abuse. Take the knife, thrust the knife, watch the blood. Disconnect. Follow instructions. Don't feel.

In my recovery, this part of the abuse is the most painful, it carries the deepest wounds. How can a person overcome the evil of having killed another human being?

People say, "Maybe it wasn't a real human. Maybe they made you think it was real." That may be the case, but I will never know for sure. It *could* have been real flesh, real blood.

People say, "It's not your fault. You were a child. You were forced to do it." That is true. But the hands that held the knife are my hands. These hands—these hands that I write with, that I eat with.

These hands that touch my spouse and tend my garden. These hands carry the stain of death.

Now that I am reconnecting to myself—remembering, feeling for the first time—I am horrified by what my hands participated in. Sometimes I want to disown, disconnect those parts of my body that participated in the abuse of other people. I wish I could cut off my hands, get a hand transplant. I wish I could somehow be cleansed from the stains. I wish I could pretend it wasn't true and ignore the feelings.

I want forgiveness from the souls who died. I want freedom from that sickening shame that lives inside of me.

From where does healing come?

The Holy Innocents—Baby Angels

I felt some connection to the children who died. Often I wondered why they died and I did not. Sometimes I wished I had been one of them rather than one left behind, forced to go through the horrors of having lived. A wise, kind minister told me about the holy innocents, the babies who were slain by King Herod's soldiers in his attempt to kill the baby Jesus. [This story is found in Matt. 2:16–18.] The clergyman told me that he thought those children were now with God, that they were like the holy innocents in the story. And he told me that I was one of those holy innocents, also; that what my body was forced to do was done by the abusers, not by me. He said that I was connected to God, to the Good, in a very special way because I suffered because of others' hatred of God.

At his words, I could see the baby angels playing in the light. I felt their forgiveness. And I felt some measure of assurance that I could let go of the guilt that I carried.

Healing Touch

Upon the recommendation of my doctor and my therapist, I began to receive massage from a massage therapist. The first time she worked on my hands, I had a flashback. In my mind, I could see blood on my hands. I felt overwhelmed with horror and sadness that my hands were being treated so tenderly. They did not deserve such tenderness.

I brought myself back from the flashback and told my massage therapist what I was seeing and feeling. As we talked about my hands, I began to understand that they were a part of me—not separate beings operating on their own. I began to see that they were not evil, that they had been used, like I had been used, by the abusers. I made the first step toward being able to accept them as a part of me and allowing them to receive love and comfort in the form of healing touch.

The Paradox of Being Alive

I don't know that there will ever be total freedom from the horror that was my childhood. I have come very far in the healing of my body, my spirit, my wounds.

But I cannot recover the part of me that died with those others. I don't know, exactly, what was lost—my innocence, a certain level of trust in human beings, a sense that God is in control of things. I live with a sort of survivor guilt, not knowing why I was spared death, wondering whether my living is my punishment for having killed others.

When I remember the knife, the blood, the terror, I cannot imagine ever being free from that pain. At the same time, that pain in me is the tribute to those innocent children who died. And my living is a sort of sign that even though the abusers tried, they did not kill my soul.

The experiences of my life, my days of living, embody the paradox of good and evil. And if my life has a purpose, that purpose grows out of my life experiences. I am who I am today because of what has happened to me. And wherever I am led in the rest of my life, I am forever connected to those baby angels who play in the light of God's love.

CHAPTER EIGHT

Reclaiming Ritual as an Agent of Healing

A ritual is any act we come to with love and reverence, an action that sheds light on the sacred qualities of our lives.
—Shea Darian, *Seven Times the Sun*

Ritual Is Not a Bad Word

Just because we were ritually abused does not mean we must abandon all aspects of ritual in our lives. Early in my journey of recovery, a friend reminded me that human beings were using ritual long before the cult had begun.

The theologian Frederick Buechner says that ritual is "A wedding. A handshake. A kiss. A coronation. A parade. A dance. A meal. A graduation. A Mass. A ritual is the performance of an intuition, the rehearsal of a dream, the playing of a game."[1]

We human beings were created with a sense of ritual, of sacrament. The earliest cultures of humanity used ritual to convey a sense of continuity in their lives. Through the ages, humans have used ritual to mark time, to recognize special events in their lives and the world, and to acknowledge the transcendent (that mystery which is greater than we are).

We have choice in our healing process. We can choose to reclaim and redefine the word or concept of ritual and incorporate it into our lives in a healthy way.

Ritual is not a bad word. Rituals were used to abuse us, but rituals themselves are not inherently bad or destructive. We can reclaim the use and positive power of ritual as a gift to us as human beings.

You probably already observe some rituals in a positive way. You might observe the celebration of birthdays and sobriety dates. You might have a bedtime ritual such as reading stories before going to sleep. You may observe particular religious/cultural holidays, death anniversaries, or the coming of your favorite season of the year.

We need ritual as a part of our lives. It is a part of our lives whether we call it ritual or not. We need it to mark time, to commemorate events, to recognize moments, to celebrate lives.

Ritual as a Healing Agent

One way to rid the word *ritual* of its negative connotations is to intentionally use ritual as a part of the healing process. In fact, using ritual is a powerful experience for ritual abuse survivors.

- It can provide stability—as in having an opening and a closing ritual for individual or group therapy.
- It can provide courage and strength—as in creating a special gathering with friends before a person leaves for a trip or for treatment.
- It can provide celebration times—as in marking a sobriety date, a birthday one was not supposed to have lived through, or the anniversary of the beginning of memories (a chance to look back and see how far one has come).
- Ritual can be created to help us let go of family members or to divorce cult members to whom we were married.
- Ritual can be created to welcome and orient new kids to the system. Or it can be used as a part of abreactive work to help heal the parts of us that took the abuse.

Reclaiming ritual is healing because by using it, we are taking back some of the power that was taken from us. When we redefine and reclaim the events, the seasons, the calendar dates that were used to hurt us, we are saying *no* to the abuse and saying *yes* to creating our own lives.

Use your imagination and creativity to help you think of ways to reclaim ritual in your life—or to recognize the ways you are already using it.

Consider the following questions:

1. In what ways do I use ritual today? Are there some things that I like to do the same way each time I do them? (Think about times when you are happy, times when you are sad.)
2. How do I make note of special days? (My birthday, Fridays or weekends, sobriety date?)
3. What do I do to help myself recover from a flashback or difficult memory? What are actions or messages that help the child parts feel better?
4. Are any of the things I have listed above types of healing rituals? Are there special actions (or rituals) I can add to some of these situations that will enhance my healing?
5. Make a list of events that are special, meaningful, or life-giving for you. Think about ways that you observe these occasions. Are there rituals you would like to add to these events?

Examples of Using Healing Rituals

Several examples follow of ways in which ritual abuse survivors have used ritual to enhance their healing.

The Garden of Courage and Remembrance

This is the story of the creation of a flower garden to celebrate survivors and memorialize persons who did not survive abuse by a satanic cult. The garden is called "The Garden of Courage and Remembrance."

The Idea

I can't remember exactly when the idea came to me that what I needed was a flower garden to remember all the people that didn't make it out of the cult. I think it was sometime around my birthday, when I was struggling to overcome the programming that said I had to die before I turned thirty-four.

On the day of my thirty-fourth birthday, my treatment team of therapists/people who care/helpers had a birthday party for me. We had strawberry frozen yogurt and fruit drink and Snoopy bowls. We celebrated that I was alive, that I had made it through the storm.

I took each of them a red rose to symbolize the life that they bring to me and to others like me—a symbol of my gratitude for all the care and hope and life they had given to me. And I had a white rose for me, to help me remember the people who did not make it—those who were killed, those who killed themselves, those who just couldn't make it any longer.

I decided that I needed a garden with a white rose bush. A garden to memorialize all those people who died at the hands of the cult—a memorial garden. I thought about it from time to time, and as I thought about it, I began to feel an urgency about it. I needed the garden to be a part of my healing journey. It was an inner feeling—I didn't know what shape it would take or what it would accomplish.

Preparing the Space

I didn't know where to put it. There needed to be some dirt there (that's tough in our yard). I wanted it to be close to the house so I could see it. It had to be in the sun enough of the day that I could grow a rose bush.

There was a big gravel pile underneath one of the two cedar trees nearest the house. One of my friends who is a ritual abuse survivor had regularly asked to be assured that no one was buried there. I decided that was the place for it. It was in full view from the chair where I spent my morning meditation time.

But first, we had to move the gravel pile. We moved the gravel pile to the back yard via the pick-up truck. (Gravel doesn't load well with a shovel, but it unloads a lot quicker than it loads.)

Once the gravel pile was moved, we had to decide what shape to make the garden. Not square—too boring. But not round—too many triggers. We were going to buy landscaping timbers. Then we realized that we had a pile of rocks left over from when our house was built. My significant other helped decide on a shape by laying out rocks on the ground. The shape is not a circle, but it has nice curves and a fluid, whole feeling.

The next task was digging up the grass that was where the garden would be. Under where the gravel had been, there was no grass, so I dug up sod from the new garden area and moved it to the bare spot. The extra sod went to the compost pile. Then I loosened the whole area with a spading fork and pulled out pieces of slate and rocks of all sizes. This was the most frustrating part of the whole process, but I decided that it was symbolically appropriate that my garden should have lots of rocks in it.

Once the ground was worked soft, I put in layers of peat moss, sand, bone meal, composted manure, and dirt. The dirt had to be moved to the garden—again via the pick-up truck— from a pile in the backyard. It took two truckloads and lots of sweat. More layers of rock were set around the edges of the garden to raise it. Then on top, I put my compost pile, which had been transforming over the winter as I had been doing my inner work.

Preparing the space for the garden was hard, strenuous, frustrating work. But even that part provided its own kind of healing. As I worked, I sweated out feelings of rage, shame, sadness. Sometimes I sang to me and the kids: "Sing God a simple song,

Lauda, Laude."[2] Or, "Hush, hush, somebody's calling my name. . . . Sounds like Freedom, somebody's calling my name. . . . I'm so glad trouble don't last always. . . . Oh my Lord, oh my Lord what shall I do?"[3]

Sometime during the preparation of the space, I began to see the garden as more than a memorial for those who had died. I saw it also as a place to honor and celebrate those who had survived. The garden should also be a place where my inner children can enjoy the colors of life, where I can celebrate their courage, their creativity, and their strength. Instead of "The Memorial Garden," I began to call it "The Garden of Courage and Remembrance."

I decided that I wanted to investigate what the name "Courage and Remembrance" would be in Hebrew. *Chazak v'Zicaron* is the Hebrew name. *Chazak* (courage) has the same root as Hezekiah. *Zicaron* (remember) is related in its root to Zechariah. The Hebrew name had great meaning to me since I have always identified with the people of Israel and their struggles.

Preparing for the Dedication

I chose four special people to join me for the naming and dedication of the garden: my two primary helpers and my two best friends.

The time was set for 8:30 to 9:30 on a Monday morning in May. My helpers were to arrive at 8:30 and stay for an hour. I planned the schedule for the morning—guests' arrival, tour of the house and the chickadee and bluebird nests, the dedication of the garden, tea and visiting, and the departure.

I transplanted some of my perennials from my other flower garden—coreopsis, gaillardia (Indian blanket), and daisies (my mother's favorite flower). I purchased three pink azaleas and planted them along the back of the garden. And I bought the white rose bush.

I had envisioned a bench under the cedar tree next to the garden, but as the inner kids became more involved, it was evident that the bench would be a swing hanging from the tree. We bought a swing and hung it two evenings before the dedication.

As I planned the actual ritual for the dedication, I became worried that I might be reenacting a cult ritual from my past, or at least reenacting my role as priestess in the cult. I called one of my helpers and shared my plans with her. She said it sounded healthy to her and encouraged me to reclaim my gifts and skills and rights to have ritual as a part of my life.

The night before the dedication, I dug the hole where the rose bush would be planted, prepared the soil to go around the rose, and set out the tools for the planting. The rose bush hole looked like a grave, so I covered it with a piece of tin.

The Ritual of Dedication

Right before my guests arrived, the kids asked if their bear could sit on the swing with them for the dedication. I decided that would be appropriate, so that's where they were.

The five of us gathered at the garden. It was cool and over-cast that morning, and the colors of spring were vivid.

I said a few words of gratitude for the presence of these important people in my life. Then we began the ritual with the naming of the garden. I had recently heard again the story of Jacob sleeping with his head on a rock and having a vision, then pouring oil on a rock and naming the place Bethel (house of God). I had put a big rock in the garden to represent the courage. I poured oil on that rock and named the place "The Garden of Courage and Remembrance," *Chazak v'Zicaron*. The oil was in an olive wood jar that a special friend had brought me from Israel.

I asked my helper to put some oil on my forehead to symbol-ize that the garden was a place of healing for me . . . a place of healing of my wounds and the wounds of the kids inside of me.

Then we planted the rose bush in memory of those who died. I talked about how the hole had reminded me of a grave and how the act of planting a rose bush there is symbolic of the transformation that we are participating in—death to life. I set the rose bush in the hole, and everyone helped shovel the dirt around it. Then I asked my other helper to read a prayer for planting that I had written.

My helpers brought gifts for the garden. A terra-cotta bunny for the kids like the one in my therapist's garden; some shooting star and some dwarf irises. And forget-me-nots—for remembering not only those who died, but also those like me who are reclaiming our lives.

We chose the place for these special gifts and planted them as a part of the ritual. Then we had a time for other words to be said. I cannot reproduce those words. But I could feel healing happening inside of me as we stood together in that moment of the Spirit. It was a moment of healing—a spiritual experience.

We went in for tea and conversation and to warm up. But the healing was still going on inside of me.

The Garden Grows

As I drove into work that morning, I felt like my car was floating. So much power in that ritual of healing!

I've received more gifts for the garden, and I've spent much healing time in it. The first white rose bloom came a couple of weeks later. It is as if every time it blooms, I can let go of a little more.

I have used the swing and the garden when I have needed to sit somewhere and grieve—after a difficult flashback, when I bump up against the wall of pain.

Later that summer, two of my survivor friends from out of town were visiting. They added their own gifts to the garden, remembering the ones who had died in their presence.

I sense that the garden will be dedicated over and over again as I share it with the special people in my life. It is indeed a garden of courage and remembrance. And it is a garden of healing and hope and promise. (And it has *lots* of flowers for the kids. They never got to see pretty colors on the dark side.) The garden belongs to more than me. I share it with all those who need to heal. And I continue my healing every time I water it or pull a weed or trim off a dead bloom.

RECLAIMING SEASONAL RITUALS

For most "normal" people, the full moon is a symbol of romance, of beauty, of marking time or listening to the rhythm of creation. But for many ritual abuse survivors, the full moon is a reminder of endless rituals and horrible abuse.

And so, also, with other seasonal rituals. Their meanings are corrupted by the perpetration of abuse and they become painful reminders rather than connections with life.

Each survivor may choose the challenge of reclaiming the full moon, the celebration of the change of seasons (the solstice or equinox), cultural or religious holidays (Christmas, Thanksgiving, Easter, etc.).

One survivor used the American Indian tradition of naming the full moons to help her reclaim them for her life.

A Full Moon Calendar

I read a book called *The Indian Way: Learning to Communicate with Mother Earth.*[4] It contained suggestions for helping the earth and for living in harmony with nature. The format of the book was structured around the full moons, and I learned that some American Indian traditions have specific names for each full moon.

I painted a moon calendar with a picture of nature representing each full moon. When I see a full moon now, I try to remember the name for the moon and the reminder it gives me of the richness of the earth and the passing of time.

The names for each full moon in the book are listed below. But we can make up our own names for the full moons based on our own experiences.

First Moon (January)—The Moon When the Snow Blows like Spirits in the Wind

Second Moon (February)—The Moon of Frost Sparkling in the Sun

Third Moon (March)—The Moon of Buffalo Dropping Their Calves

Fourth Moon (April)—The Moon of Ice Breaking in the River

Fifth Moon (May)—The Moon When the Ponies Shed Their Shaggy Hair

Sixth Moon (June)—The Moon When the Hot Weather Begins

Seventh Moon (July)—The Moon When the Buffalo Bellow

Eighth Moon (Late July)—The Moon When the Chokecherries Begin to Ripen

Ninth Moon (August)—The Moon of Geese Shedding Their Feathers

Tenth Moon (September)—The Moon of Drying Grass

Eleventh Moon (October)—The Moon of Falling Leaves

Twelfth Moon (November)—The Moon When the Rivers Start to Freeze

Thirteenth Moon (December)—The Moon of Popping Trees[5]

Think about the different months of the year where you live. What is your favorite part of each month? Make your own moon calendar and name the moons based on your happy or significant experiences. For instance, if you like to ski, name January as The Moon of the Snow Skis. If your favorite flower is the daffodil, name March (or whichever month the daffodils bloom) The Moon of Yellow Daffodils. If you are a baseball fan, name October as The Moon of the World Series. Name your birthday month The Moon of Birthday Presents.

SPEAKING OUT TO GOD: A LITURGY FOR SURVIVORS OF ABUSE

This liturgy is a script designed to allow survivors to enact a trial in which God is charged with inaction and complacency in the survivors' abuse. It is inspired by the writing of Elie Wiesel, a Jewish survivor of the Holocaust. In Wiesel's book *The Gates of the Forest*, the author recounts through a character in the book a *D'in Torah* that was held at Auschwitz. A *D'in Torah* is a trial in which God is the defendant. In Wiesel's book, God is indicted and found guilty for the crime of murder.[6]

It is often difficult for us survivors of abuse to work through the anger we feel about God's absence, indifference, or powerlessness in our abuse. In order to be able to heal spiritually, feelings toward God must be acknowledged and expressed. This liturgy is designed to invite the expression of these feelings.

Within the Jewish tradition, it is said that it is acceptable to say anything to God as long as you say it on behalf of humanity and the world. Thus, expressions of anger against God are appropriate and not uncommon.

In "Speaking Out to God," the concept of the *D'in Torah* is adapted for use in the healing of survivors of ritual abuse. Adapt the script to fit your situation and your needs.

Preparation. Think about the place you would like to hold your liturgy. (Examples: Your therapist's office, a church building, your home, a park.) Who would you like to ask to be present? (Other survivors of ritual abuse, a clergy person or representative of your religion or faith, your therapist or other helpers.) How would you like to change the words, order, or content of the liturgy to fit your needs and situation?

If it seems too much for you to organize, ask a friend or helper to assist you in planning and carrying out the liturgy. Ask someone to read the parts of Narrator, Judge, and Representative, and give them a copy. You can have one person read them all, or you can ask several people to be involved in the reading. You read the parts labeled Survivor.

Prepare for your support during the liturgy and after the liturgy is over. Ask someone who will be present to be your support person during the liturgy. Make plans ahead of time to be with supportive people and to process the experience afterwards. (Read the section on "Processing the Experience of the Liturgy" at the end of this chapter.) Schedule time with your therapist, helper, or spiritual director after the liturgy to talk about and express your feelings.

This activity is for your healing. Shape the setting, content, and participants to your liking. Remember that it is your liturgy and you can stop it at any time. You have permission to do and say what you need in order to heal.

The Liturgy: Speaking Out to God

Participants: The survivor, the narrator, the judge, the representative, other witnesses.

Narrator: We come here together as supporters and witnesses on behalf of our friend, [name of survivor]. As a community of healing, we share the power to speak out our words of anger, sadness, and grief. We collectively witness to the injustices that [name of survivor] has endured and we stand with [her/him] as we call God to accountability.

We claim the tradition that says that God will hear the cries of the innocent and will listen to that which is spoken on behalf of humanity and the world. We speak for the innocent, the vulnerable, the wounded, the children. We require the attention of God, the Creator, the One who speaks justice, but who did not intervene in the injustice in the life of [name of survivor]. Let the liturgy begin.

Judge: This trial shall come to order. What charges are brought against God, and who brings them?

Survivor: I bring charges. I call upon God to answer my questions, to listen to my charges, to hear my arguments. I charge God with complacency in my abuse [add any other charges here] and the abuse of many others at the hands of ritual abusers.

Judge: Who stands as representative to hear the charges?

Representative: I stand as representative. I listen to what you have to say, on behalf of the One you charge. I bring no harm or threat to you. You may speak whatever needs to be said. For it is true that whatever you have to say is acceptable as long as you say it on behalf of humankind and the world—and you are part of humankind.

Judge (to the survivor): What evidence do you bring to support your charges?

Survivor: I bring this evidence:

Inaction: You were not there when I was being tortured and abused. You say you protect the weak, but you did not protect me. You stood by and allowed me to be raped, tortured, exposed to inhumane acts. You allowed the abusers to kill innocent people. You allowed your name and your beliefs to be used against me. [Add other charges here.]

Feelings: I am angry, disappointed, confused, and lonely; full of despair, rage, and feelings of abandonment. [Add other feelings here.]

Questions: I ask why you would allow these horrors to happen? Why did you not stop the torture and the killings? How can you say that you are for the weak when you allow such things to happen? Who am I to turn to for help if it is not you, the Protector and Justice Maker? [Add other questions here.]

Judge: Are there other witnesses who would like to speak?

[Here others may speak their feelings or thoughts as witnesses.]

Judge (to the representative): What have you to say to the witness of these people, their thoughts, feelings, and evidence?

Representative: I hear all that has been spoken. I respond with sadness, compassion, and anger at the injustices that you describe. I witness and testify that your words and your feelings have been heard and felt by the One I represent. Your burden is shared by that One who, though you may not have felt it, stood by you in your abuse and was on *your* side and not on the side of the abusers.

I wish for the power to reshape your life to exclude the horrors that you endured. I am humbled that you stand before me alive, aware, and angry. I call for the cessation of any such acts by any part of humanity. I call for the support of all witnesses to testify to the truth of this abuse, to educate the unknowing, to call to accountability those who perpetrate evil, to listen with compassion to survivors of abuse. The testimony you bring asks little and much: that torture, cruelty, rape, and murder be stopped. That those who commit such acts be called to accountability. You are a witness to truth and to peace and to justice. May your life be blessed. [The representative may make additional comments here.]

Judge: Having heard the evidence and response of these witnesses and the defendant, I find God guilty as charged. (To the survivor) What is it that you would demand as reparation for your wounds?

Survivor: I ask God and the court to listen to the cries of the wounded, to have compassion for the children, to speak the truth to all who will hear. I demand the following: [here the survivor lists his/her requirements for reparation].

Judge: The demands of the survivor are duly heard and humbly accepted. I charge each one here to carry out the witness inherent in knowing the truth of this survivor. I remind each of you to speak the truth, to stand by with compassion in the face of evil, to protect the vulnerable. [Here the judge may list other requirements of the defendant or the witnesses. Also, the judge may make additional comments.] If there are no other statements, I hereby declare this trial to be completed.

[Silence]

Narrator: The trial is completed. God has heard the charges and received judgment. We witnesses have been charged with our duties of responsibility. No amount of compassion can change what has happened in the life of [name of survivor] and the others who were abused. But we are all stronger because of [her/him] and the witness to justice that [he/she] brings.

We thank those who participated in this liturgy, and we acknowledge their real roles in the life of [name the survivor]. You are no longer judge, representative, witness, and narrator. You are friends, supporters, and helpers. Before we go, do you have further reflections, observations, or thoughts that you would like to share?

[The friends of the survivor may share other thoughts here.]

[The survivor may share thoughts, needs, feelings, reflections here.]

[If there is need for further discussion, processing, or supportive action for the survivor or any of the participants, it may happen here.]

Narrator: Let us go from here, witnesses to truth and justice. [The group may join together in the serenity prayer, other community prayer, or a time of silence for those who still suffer.]

Processing the Experience of the Liturgy

Such liturgies as this can be powerful in our lives. It is important to spend time to feel the feelings of the experience. This processing may be done as a part of the liturgy. Or you may choose to spend some intentional time with your therapist or helper to integrate your feelings and learnings and move forward from the experience. Write about the experience and how you felt. Ask yourself whether there are further things you need to say to God or to hear from a representative of God.

Here are some questions that may help you in your processing of the experience:

1. What were your feelings during the liturgy? What are your feelings now?
2. Name your next steps for healing.
3. Make a list of your spiritual losses.
4. Which losses would you like to process further?
5. Write down any unanswered spiritual questions that you have.
6. Make a list of the questions you would like to discuss with someone. With whom would you like to discuss them?

From a Child Survivor of Ritual Abuse

This narrative is from Claire, a thirteen-year-old survivor of ritual abuse. She writes about herself, "I run cross-country, play violin and piano. I love to read. I am Episcopalian. I love to go to church and youth activities."

The abuse happened to me in a church setting while my parents were worshiping. I was about six or seven when the abuse took place. The child care workers would take us to the woods and to a large mansion and abuse us. This happened for several years.

My family went away for a year to another country. When I returned to this country, I was sure the abuse hadn't happened to me. When I went to counseling I would say, "No, it didn't happen." Then I would say, "Yes, maybe it happened." Then I would begin to see things in my mind (like people getting abused), but I didn't let my feelings bother me at first.

The first time we were abused in the woods, I think I knew what happened; but mentally and emotionally I blocked it so it wasn't so painful. After church I went home and really didn't remember anything. Sometimes when the abuse was taking place I found myself looking down (like an out-of-body experience) and looking at the abuse taking place. I didn't want to feel it happening, so I just watched everyone else being abused.

Going for Therapy

I went to therapy for about two and one-half years. I didn't want to go at first. But if I hadn't gone, I would still be saying that the abuse didn't happen. And I would be more perfectionistic than I am now, and would always be seeing the wrong in everything.

I don't need to go to counseling anymore. I can be my own counselor. I have learned how to relate to my problems. If I have a problem and don't know what it's about, most likely it's about something that happened at the time of the abuse. I also have to be careful that I don't blame everything on the abuse.

I used to think I was a good Christian (on a scale of one to ten, maybe I was a five or six). But after this experience, I realized that it was God who healed me, and I really got to know who God is. God's not just someone in the sky. God is there for you. I know that if someone ever came to me and told me that a problem like this happened to them, I would believe them.

The abuse also made me grow up faster at first. But when I realized what happened, I shrunk back down. Now I'm growing at a regular pace.

When we killed the babies and the animals and were forced to do things to other people, I felt it was my fault and that God didn't love me. Nobody loved me, and I was a bad person and should go to jail. But then I realized that it wasn't me who was bad; it was those who abused me.

About the Abusers

My attitude toward the abusers is that it's better to pray for them than to stay angry at them, because being mad at them isn't going to change anything. Being put in jail may help them to not hurt other people, but they still aren't sorry for what they did. If they were really sorry they would learn to love God and not do bad things.

If the wicked can ask for forgiveness, then we won't see them fall. This Bible verse has been meaningful to me: "No one who conceals transgressions will prosper, but one who confesses and forsakes them will obtain mercy" (Prov. 28:13). You can't hold bad things inside, but have to ask for forgiveness.

Proverbs 26:25–26 says, "When an enemy speaks graciously, do not believe it, for there are seven abominations concealed within; though hatred is covered with guile, the enemy's wickedness will be exposed in the assembly." This reminds me that during the abuse, the perpetrators went to church like everyone else. They seemed to be like normal people (because they probably were multiple personalities). They seemed to love everyone else. But God really knows this person's heart, whether it is bad or good.

"When the wicked are in authority, transgression increases, but the righteous will look upon their downfall" (Prov. 29:16). Even if you think everyone is against you and everyone is doing something you or God would think is wrong, God is always there with you. If there are six hundred on their side, God is going to have one thousand on your side.

CHAPTER NINE

Healing Our Spiritual Selves

i found god in myself / & i loved her / i loved her fiercely
—Ntozake Shange, *for colored girls who have considered suicide/
when the rainbow is enuf*

Spiritual Abuse and Woundedness

Spiritual abuse is perhaps the greatest wound of a ritual abuse survivor. Pia Mellody defines spiritual abuse as "experiences that distort, retard, or otherwise interfere with a child's spiritual development."[1] For the ritual abuse survivor, the spiritual self is one of the most injured and the most difficult areas to heal.

Any kind of abuse of a child by an adult creates aspects of spiritual woundedness. When a child is hurt by someone on whom he or she is dependent for nurture or sustenance, this abuse of power creates confusion for that child. All children have a tendency to see adults and caregivers as Godlike—all-powerful, omnipotent, omnipresent. When this same Godlike figure perpetrates abuse, the child's trust in others is destroyed. The one who was supposed to protect the child abused him or her. The child's trust and relationship with a higher power is also affected.

Children may think that the abuser *is* God, that God actually hurt them. In cases of satanic rituals, the cult may intentionally create the illusion that God, Jesus, or some other religious figure is abusing the child. Children may be given verbal messages that they are being hurt because God does not like them or because they were bad and God is angry.

Adult survivors carry the spiritual wounds explicitly given them in childhood. Wounds surface as the survivor moves through the stages of growth in which he or she develops a sense of self, other, and the spiritual. As adult survivors uncover their abuse, they uncover spiritual questions and spiritual woundedness. Questions form: "Where was God? How could a loving God let this happen to me? How could God let parents do these things to their children? Why doesn't God take responsibility for what God has created? Was God participating in the abuse? Am I being punished for something?"

Survivors may be angry and disillusioned with God and religion. Many ritual abusers appeared to be religious in their everyday lives. They were upstanding members of the congregation, pastors and priests, deacons and church leaders. Ritual abuse survivors call the church to accountability, asking why someone did not stop the abuse. Some survivors feel that the church is responsible by its complacency and lack of advocacy. Some survivors believe that God or the church was actually involved in the abuse and can never be trusted again.

 Survivors' memories of specific abusive rituals based on the sacraments of the organized church increase confusion. To have been subjected to ritual abuse means, by definition, to have been abused in ritualistic ways. This childhood ritualistic abuse is easily confused with any ritual-oriented activities of the survivor's life in the present. Furthermore, satanic cults use rituals of the Christian church as a basis for their satanic rituals. These activities then become uncomfortable and may trigger painful memories for survivors. Thus, activities such as twelve-step meetings, worship services of organized religious groups, or graduation ceremonies become difficult experiences.

All of these consequences add up to scarred selves, shattered trust in people and in God, and deep spiritual woundedness.

"Why Do I Need Spirituality?"

Given all that ritual abuse survivors have gone through, it is valid to ask, "Why do I need spirituality?" It seems as though contact with the spiritual has added wound upon wound to the life of the survivor.

It may be that people do not need a sense of the spirit in order to heal and become whole. Each survivor's healing experience is unique.

However, there is something special about survivors of ritual abuse who lived through the abuse and are living through the re-membering of the abuse. This "something special" may be a sense of life, a sense of hope, a sense of light that was never squelched through all the pain and hurt and cruelty and evil.

What if we could see the spark of that "something special" which lives inside of every ritual abuse survivor? What would it look like? What would it be? What if we could know what it was that kept that person alive when others died? What if we could understand why that person is remembering and healing rather than going back to perpetrate more abuse?

What can we call that spark of hope, that sense of tenacious life, that something special? Just maybe we can call it spirituality, the spirit, a sense of something within and beyond the self.

If we call it spirituality, then it includes more than what is traditionally considered spiritual. The place of the spirit is that part of us that likes to watch the sun come up, that loves to play with puppies, that wants to be near the ocean. The center of our spirituality is that part within us which shelters life. It sheltered life within us even when death and destruction were all around us. It continues to nurture life today as we remember our childhood abuse and heal from it. By healing, we are saying yes to life. That *yes* is the spirit of life inside of us.

Perhaps the question is not "Why do I need spirituality?" Perhaps the essential question is "Do I accept the parts of me that nurture life?" "Do I acknowledge that I am a living, spiritual being?" "How can I describe in my own way the parts of me that shelter life, spirit, hope, [fill in your own word]?"

Healing the Spiritual Parts of Ourselves

Healing our spiritual wounds is a slow, ongoing process. Like our growth and healing in other areas, we progress by moving ever deeper into the wounded places, uncovering the outer layers first. Like peeling away the layers of an onion, we begin first in the areas easiest to reach and then move to the inner, tenderer areas when we are ready. We pay close attention to the areas of hurt—we observe them, listen to the pain, learn the lessons of the pain, and move into new patterns or ways of thinking as we feel comfortable. We do not need to rush the process. Healing from wounds takes time; it has its own timetable.

INTERNAL SPIRITUAL HELPERS

Every ritual abuse survivor has an inner part that somehow stayed connected to life even in the midst of torture and death. This part was there throughout the abuse and, though buried deep inside, never lost a sense of the spiritual, the holy. Bernard Bush has observed that ritual abuse survivors have a part within that is a "mystical" part.[2] It nurtured life within us throughout our abuse and in our remembering.

One survivor described this part as "the Keeper of the Spirit," explaining:

> The Keeper of the Spirit made sure that my spirit, my essence, was always safe. My spirit was wrapped in a cloth bundle. Whenever one of the kids had to go out and take some abuse, the other kids and the Keeper made sure that my spirit was safe and hidden and

couldn't be touched by the perpetrators. Then when that kid came back, the Keeper would take care of the kid until all the wounds were healed.

It may have many names: the strong one, the keeper of the spirit, the healer, the mystic, the grandparent, the wise one. Whatever we call the part, we can assist in its healing by seeking that part of us, inviting it out, befriending it, nurturing it, and assisting it to develop further in our life.[3] Just as we get to know the inner children within us, we can get to know the inner helper, the inner wise one, the inner mystic. The mystical part had few allies and little encouragement during our early lives. As we befriend and nurture the spiritual within us, that part comes alive and offers back to us its life-giving gifts.

We can seek that part within by asking ourselves if anyone inside knows the wise one. Ask, "Who is the one who helps heal the others?" Think of your own characteristics that have helped you in your survival. Are they connected with that life-nurturing part of you? Draw a picture of your inner strength or spirituality. Does this part of you have a name? Does it have a relationship with other parts of you?

As you identify the part within, the place inside of you where your spiritual strength resides, begin to get to know it better and help support and nurture it. Ask inside whether there are any ways that you can better support that spiritual part of yourself. Pay attention to the ways that part of you assists in your healing, and affirm it. Share your gratitude for the life-giving strength that has been carried by that part of you.

This strong one within has a natural longing for life and healing. It is wise beyond years. It knows about pain and healing and spirit. It may be the place where our connection with a higher power resides. It guides us in the healing journey if we give it room to do so.

Wendy's "Strong One"

One of my personalities is not a kid like most of the others. She is ageless and has been around since the beginning of my abuse. My other kids call her "The Strong One" and they respect and love her very much. She has spoken to my therapist several times as an equal, not a patient. She knows everything there is to know about my system and has been an instrumental part of my healing. She is a great comfort, a wise internal helper who knows what I need to do to heal. We consider her the core self; and it is her strength that has pulled us through the abuse and the recovery of memories.

The Wounded Children Within

We are all very familiar with the wounded children within us. These are the parts of us that we know very well. They give us memories, they send us painful feelings, they demand our attention and our care.

We may be less familiar with the ways that we can work with these wounded children as we heal our spirituality. But learning how to assist in the spiritual healing of our inner selves is essential to our healing as a whole.

Some people believe that children, because of their age and innocence, are naturally more open and receptive to the spiritual. For some, the higher power lives within the child. It may be that the children within us hold the key for our spiritual healing and the recovery of our spirituality.

In addition, our process of healing from trauma includes the healing of each part of us. If the child parts of us were recipients of spiritual abuse, then these same children need help to heal from that spiritual abuse.

AGE-LEVEL UNDERSTANDINGS

Children of different ages and development understand things differently. As we work with the various ages within us, it is important to remember that these parts represent varying abilities to think, reason, and understand. We do not have to be child development experts to be able to heal all the parts of ourselves.

As we learn about child development, we may find that parts of us did not develop normally because of the trauma. We may have teenage or adult parts that think of death in the same way as does an unwounded nine-year-old.

Issues that inner children face when healing spiritual wounds include beliefs about death and dying, the nature and existence of God and Satan, ethical and nonethical actions, and programming messages from the abuse. In each of these issues, it is important to hear and respond to the child's belief or question and meet the child at the level of his or her understanding. (To learn more about stages of development, refer to the resources section at the end of this book and to the chart, "Age-Level Development," in chapter 4.)

As we hear a child's beliefs, understandings, or fears, we meet the child where he or she is and talk to the child in a way that he or she can understand. The task of healing includes the same steps for each part of us: talking and being heard, identifying and correcting untrue beliefs and perceptions, comforting the hurts, speaking the truth. As each part of us works toward healing, the other parts of us benefit from that healing work.

We can be at many different places within as we engage in healing our spiritual wounds. In our adult selves, we may be ready to incorporate some spirituality back into our lives. At the same time, some of our child selves may balk at any activity that suggests spirituality. This dissonance does not mean that the system must be in consensus before one part can try a new experience. It does mean that cooperation, communication, and negotiation are important tools to use for system management.

ASSESSING OUR SPIRITUAL DEVELOPMENT

Since having many parts means that we have many perceptions and experiences, we can aid our journey of spiritual healing by gathering information about the knowledge, perspectives, and opinions of the ones within us. The following suggestions may be helpful:

1. Look over any written dialogue that you have had with various inner children and write down any insights into their spiritual perceptions and experiences. Start a list for each different alter. (For example: "Susan, six years old, is afraid of Jesus because . . .")
2. Set aside some time to ask questions of different ones and listen to their answers. Dialogue in writing or in whatever way you are most comfortable. Add the information to your lists.
3. Assess the information you have gathered from the parts inside of you. Are there programming messages that need to be overcome? Are there misperceptions that need to be corrected? Do their understandings fit with the beliefs, values, and spiritual characteristics you wish to create, reclaim, or keep? What level of understanding or development does each part reflect?
4. Make a list of the inner parts that need work and what needs to be done. Talk with your therapist, helper, or friend to make a plan for how to work with these inner parts. It may be helpful to talk with someone who knows about the spiritual development of children. Ask your therapist to help you find someone to talk with. (If you would like to read about it yourself, look in the resources section for books on children and spirituality.)

5. Don't get discouraged if there are many things that need attention. There are probably spiritual wounds in each part of us. They will take time to heal. It is okay to have many questions and to ask other for help.

LETTERS TO GOD

Writing letters to a higher power can be a helpful tool for healing our spiritual wounds—for our adult as well as our child parts. We can say whatever we need to in a letter to a higher power. We can learn the level of understanding and the questions of our inner children by allowing them to write letters to their higher power.

We cannot easily talk to a higher power or to God in a reciprocal way, but we can have a sort of dialogue by writing God's response to the letters. If you feel comfortable, let God write back in reply to the child within. If you are not comfortable writing on behalf of a higher power, ask a person that all of you trust to answer the letter.

The following are some examples of letters to God and God's replies:

Dear God,

How could you let this happen? How could you let us get hurt this bad?

Why did you let us lose our Mickey Mouse watch? We feel scared. We hurt a lot.

The Kids

Dear Kids,

I'm sorry your watch is lost. You didn't do anything wrong, and you're not going to get in trouble. I promise.

I'm sorry you got hurt so badly. I know you feel scared today, but I will be there with you. I will stay with you in your rooms and help protect you. You will be safe today. I care about you. I hold you in the sacred place in my heart. I hold you safely. I loved you before you were born.

Love,
God

Dear God,

We want a mommy. Why can't you get us one? Why did you make my mommy go away? We feel really lonely and scared. They said if we prayed to you that you wouldn't listen, cause you hate us.

Denise and Carol

Dear Denise and Carol, little ones,

They lied to you. You are my daughters, my blessed children. You may feel alone, but you are not alone. I live deep inside your heart. Can you feel me there? . . . It feels like a warm tickle, you say? Yes, that is where I live inside of you. Your biological mother is gone. And you were alone and not taken care of. I am sad for your pain. I was sad when you were being hurt. I understand if you do not believe me or trust me. But I will never leave you. I will always live inside of you.

Love,
God

Dear God,

Do you live inside us, too?

Ellie and Lisa

Dear Ellie and Lisa,

I live inside you, too. You are my daughters. And I am very proud of you. You can call on me any time.

Love,
God

7

Dear God,

Today we remembered about being punished for going to church. We hurt really, really bad. We wanted to die. We didn't think we could make it, and we didn't want to. How come you let Jesus die and not us? How come we have to hurt so much and you won't let us die? We feel mad at you. You're not being very nice.

Ocean

Dear Ocean,

I get really sad when I hear that you want to die. I feel really sad that I could not stop the killing. I'm sorry you got hurt and that other children got hurt. And I don't want you or others to have to die today. I want you to be free. I know sometimes it feels the same as it did when you were little. But the hurt you feel today is a part of the healing that will make you free.

I know it is hard to understand all of this, because the bad people told you lots of lies and hurt you really badly. But I didn't want you to die then, and I don't want you to die now. I didn't want anyone to die at the hands of the cult, but I cannot stop people from the actions they choose.

I want you to remember that there are lots of people who want you to stay alive today. It's really okay for you to be mad at me. I can take it. It is not okay to kill or harm yourself. I want you to stay whole and be gentle and stay alive.

I love you, and it will get better.

God

P.S. I didn't want Jesus to die either.

Reaching for the Light: Reclaiming Our Spirituality

If one of the "purposes" or effects of abuse was to separate us from our selves and our spirituality, then one of the purposes of healing is to reconnect us with that spirituality. We can use images that speak to our meaning and experience to help us reclaim our spiritual selves.

"Reaching for the light" is one such image that can assist us to reclaim what was lost. This image, further developed, describes the abuse as darkness and healing as the light. Important metaphors for healing might include a light that surrounds the wounded places with healing warmth, or a light that illuminates every part of the darkness and cannot be put out. Reclaiming the spiritual self involves the action of reaching toward the place of healing, the light. The spiritual self resides in the light. The parts within carried with them a spark of light that never went out, no matter how painful and horrible the abuse that went on around them.

1. What image do you carry within you as a part of your healing?
2. What image or images illustrate your journey of reclaiming your spirituality?
3. Write a description or draw a picture of your healing image(s).

FINDING THE PLACE OF GROUNDING

A first step of reclaiming our spirituality out of the brokenness is to find the place of grounding. As we go through the process of remembering our abuse, we find ourselves being cut loose, forcibly separated from every piece of our past. This internal and external exile is very painful. We find ourselves spinning through unfamiliar space, unable to hold on to anything from our past and unfamiliar with our new reality. We are stripped of our family, our childhood, our memories, our familiar roots.

Sometimes all we have left to hang on to are a couple of friends or our therapist. Having lost the trust in what we know, we lose whatever spiritual beliefs we have held. Everything we have known is called into question and must be reexamined before we can let it into our life again.

As we begin to rebuild our lives after this incredible loss, we slowly seek to rebuild trust. We test the trust that we have—in our therapist, in friends. We tentatively step out and explore trusting other safe people.

Amidst all of the rearranging and changing, we find ourselves asking endless questions about life and its meaning for us, about the presence or existence of a higher power, a greater good, a positive life force. Before we know the answers to these questions (knowing the answers may be a lifetime endeavor), we can begin recognizing the spark of life within, our spirituality, and the place of hope by exploring and recognizing the place of our grounding.

The place of grounding is where we feel anchored, where we know at some level that all will be well, where we are able to hang on to life even when we are in despair. In *for colored girls who have considered suicide / when the rainbow is enuf*, the seven women characters discover their grounding within themselves: "i found god in myself / & i loved her / i loved her fiercely."[4] Some of us can feel the grounding place somewhere in our body. Some of us see an image or picture of our grounding place. Some of us can describe what it feels like to be grounded.

Ask yourself questions about your place of grounding: "What is it that keeps me going when I feel hopeless? When do I feel the most in tune with myself, the most settled, the most confident? When I am the most centered, where in my body do I feel my life force? How do I describe the feeling when I am breathing the deepest and am the most relaxed? When I am grounded, it (looks like this, feels like this, etc.)."

Explore and describe the place(s) you are grounded. In your place or places of grounding you will begin to reclaim the center of your spirituality.

Renaming the Great Spirit / God / Higher Power / Life Force

What name do you call the great spirit, the life force within you, the power that helped you stay alive in the midst of despair, the creator that paints the sky at sunset? What name do you call the place of the spirit, the place of your grounding?

You have the freedom and choice to use the name that you feel most comfortable using. You have the freedom and choice to use no name at all. Contrary to what many of us were taught, there are many names for that greater spirit, that inner god, that higher power.

If you feel comfortable doing so, think about what name you would use for your source of life. Spirituality and a relationship with a higher power were meticulously stripped away as a part of the ritual abuse. By reclaiming your spirituality, you empower your healing. By renaming the place of your grounding, you reclaim a chunk of what was taken from you in the abuse.

There are many names for that source of life. What names would you call God? Here are some names that others have used:

Names for God

Comforter	Healer	Grandfather
Peacemaker	Great spirit	Dancing energy
Breath	Love	Maker of justice
Friend	Shepherd	Light
Wind	Life-force	Tears
Singer	Goddess	Silent one
Color	Companion	Compassion
One who blesses	Creator	Laughter
Center	Ocean	Great blanket
Sky	Darkness	Grandmother

Nurturing Our Spiritual Selves

Once we have rediscovered that spiritual place within us, how do we nurture it and encourage it to grow? Often, other people are the greatest source of spiritual encouragement and nurture.

Through spiritual friendship or spiritual direction and organized groups of spiritual folk, other people can help nurture our spiritual development.

SPIRITUAL FRIENDSHIP OR SPIRITUAL DIRECTION

As we begin to reclaim our spiritual selves, it is helpful to be able to talk with another person about our journey, our questions, and our discoveries. Within some traditions, this type of relationship—where we seek guidance or companionship on our spiritual journey—is called "spiritual friendship" or "spiritual direction."

Since we come to healing with many spiritual wounds, we have many spiritual questions. Some of our questions can be answered within our therapy work. But there may be many other questions that cannot be answered in that setting. And we may have a desire to talk with someone exclusively about spirituality. We can talk with other people in both formal and informal ways about our spiritual concerns.

You may have a desire for continuity over time in your exploration. A sponsor from a twelve-step group may be the person with whom you feel most comfortable talking about your spiritual journey. Or there may be a friend with whom you feel comfortable talking about such things. Think about the support network you have, and identify people you would like to talk to about your spiritual life.

Some of us may have the desire and opportunity to develop a more formal relationship with a spiritual director, a person with whom we contract for a relationship over time. Within this relationship, we are able to discuss spiritual questions and dilemmas. In a relationship with a spiritual director, we can receive guidance, feedback, and education about our questions, experiences, and struggles.

Most metropolitan areas have communities of people who provide spiritual direction or friendship. Look for programs that train spiritual directors or centers of study related to spiritual formation. Or ask your therapist to help you find a safe person from within the spiritual community.

Spiritual direction can come from a person with training in spirituality. Or it can come from a trusted and respected friend. The primary concern for us is intentionality—acknowledging that our spiritual journey is as important as the other journeys of our life— and taking the steps necessary to nurture our spiritual selves.

COMMUNITIES OF SPIRITUAL FOLKS

We may find communities of people to assist us in nurturing and encouraging the spiritual places within us.

Twelve-step groups. One type of community is the twelve-step group. Many of us are already familiar with the twelve-step group as we have worked to recover from various addictions and ways of coping with the pain of our abuse. The twelve-step group is helpful in its openness to each individual's concept of his or her higher power. Many of us find freedom to develop our spirituality within the flexible structure of the twelve steps. In addition, the meetings give us the opportunity to share safely with others about our spirituality and hear about the understandings and experiences of others.

Most areas host a variety of twelve-step groups, including groups for survivors of abuse. In addition, some support groups for ritual abuse survivors are being created using a twelve-step format. Talk to other survivors and therapists in your area to investigate your options for twelve-step groups.

Churches and synagogues. Another community of support is a local church or synagogue. This community of people may not be an option for some survivors. Our ritualistic abuse may be too similar to the structure, format, and make-up of the local church to be a healthy place for us.

But others of us may find that such a community offers the kind of spiritual support and nurture that we desire. Often the local church or synagogue we choose may be very different from the one in which we grew up (if we were a part of one when growing up). Sometimes, the community offers us the networking and support that we need to heal from the abuse. Gathered within the community of faith are people who can listen, believe our story, provide comfort and nurture, assist us in our spiritual growth, and lend support and friendship when we are lonely.

Those of us who had a community of faith before we began our process of healing may find that we can grow, change, question, and feel our pain within that community. At other times, we discover that we need to be associated with a different sort of community in order to meet our needs.

As we move into a community of faith, a local church, or a synagogue, we may expect some old feelings and triggers to surface. For some of us, participating in a community of faith is an activity for our adult and not for the kids inside. Wounded children often need a lot of help to overcome the triggers, symbols, and liturgies that are a part of a local church or synagogue. If that is the case, the adult part can contract with the children within to offer them an alternate activity when the adult is participating in the community. It may take some time for the healing to happen on the inside.

Whether or not the inner kids are participants, it is important to take the process at your own pace. Participating in a community of faith is a choice you have. No one except you knows whether it is the right choice for you. You can take as much time as you need to make the choice and to live into that choice in a way that is helpful and healing for you.

Mary's Spiritual Journey

My faith is fairly strong and healthy. I know and understand a lot about the true God, and I am grateful for that. But I feel this faith is shallow. I fear that it does not go deep inside me, that there are significant parts of me to which it does not penetrate. I have *lots* of fear in me about spiritual things, and I feel very lost and confused in this area. I belong to a charismatic Episcopal church and I see that I have deeply seated fear about the expression of various spiritual gifts. I can hide this fear to a degree, but every now and then an incident arises that shows me how "hung-up" I am. I know my fear is a stumbling block, but I feel very uncertain and afraid of how to deal with it.

  I also struggle with many of the Episcopal traditions. They are reminiscent of the satanic rituals, and so they trigger me. I am slowly working to feel safe in a regular worship/communion service.

I feel that this spiritual realm is a major frontier area for me to work on in my healing journey. Yet I feel daunted by it: I feel uncertain about what I need to do and how to do it, let alone where to seek help. I try to talk to God about what is going on with me and seek God's guidance.

Currently I am trying to teach my inner kids about Jesus, thinking that building positive knowledge and experiences there will help create a foundation for my faith. And I think this is helping. At other times I've consciously worked on building a new and correct image of the true God for myself.

I truly believe that *trust* is a big, big stumbling block for ritualistic abuse survivors. We were so very deeply betrayed and deceived—often by members of our own families, or the church, or both. This makes it extremely difficult for us to trust others. And it is even more difficult to really trust God, someone we can't see.

ASSESSING OUR NEEDS FOR SPIRITUAL NURTURE

There are many more ways to nurture our spiritual selves. Only a couple of examples have been named here. Just as our bodies heal when we are cut, our spirits heal from their wounds. We can assist that healing by listening to our selves and caring for them as we care for any wounded part of us. This is new language and new experience for us. It will take time and practice. If the answers—or even the questions—are not clear now, take a break and come back to them another time. Or make a commitment to check in with yourself on a regular basis and assess your needs and your progress.

1. Ask yourself, "What are my spiritual wounds?" If nothing comes right away, sit with the question awhile. Carry the question with you as you go about your daily tasks. When answers surface, write them down.
2. Ask yourself, "What are my spiritual needs?" Live with the question if you need to. Write down the answers as they come to you.
3. Ask yourself, "In what ways do I need spiritual nurture?" As you identify these needs for nurture, ask yourself what will satisfy those needs. Write down what you learn.
4. Make a list of your unanswered spiritual questions. Think of several ways in which you can pursue these questions, and choose one way to try.
5. Make a "Spiritual Self-Care Plan." Begin by defining what spiritual self care is for you. (One example is to identify someone with whom you can discuss difficult spiritual questions.) Ask your therapist, friend, or spiritual companion for ideas. Do something from the plan each week.

Patience—Slow and Easy

Spiritual healing takes time. Remember that deep wounds take time to heal. Spiritual wounds are just as deep as the wounds of the mind, emotions, and body. Assist your healing by being gentle with yourself, nurturing yourself, being patient with the healing process.

Speak kindly to yourself, not expecting yourself "to be farther along by now" or "not having this problem again." You are just where you are supposed to be. It is okay to be wherever you are, to have the questions and feelings that you have, to progress at your own pace, to take a rest when you need it. It is okay to be patient with your spiritual selves and take it slow and easy.

Love Is Real

Sister Hope is a college professor, mother, and wife. She is a survivor of nineteen years of incest and satanic ritual abuse. She enjoys reading, research, yoga, martial arts, hiking, skiing, horses, and racquetball.

The process of my recovery from ritual abuse has been one of horror. Of feeling plunged into horror, fighting its power, trying to keep from drowning. It has been a process of ungluing my words, of oiling my jaws, like Dorothy does for the Tin Man in *The Wizard of Oz.*

Much of this process has not been so much fighting horror (although it is that, too), but of finding a way to "speak" horror. What I mean here, is to "speak" horror in such a way as to speak myself *through* and *out* of the horror. Sometimes I feel as if my life were a B-minus horror flick—except far scarier than any horror movie—and I want to just reach out, flip that switch, turn it off, and go upstairs to that safe, real world, have some warm milk, and go to bed. The problem is that the real world lately does not feel safe, *is* horror; although the problem is also in the ways I deal with the abuse.

At one point in therapy, I said to my therapist, "That's it. No more. I've had enough." I just refused to do therapy. I was too tired, too inundated. So for the next three weeks, I brought my favorite movies to therapy, and we watched them together. I needed to rest, and that was okay. But after a while my therapist said to me, "The only way out of the fire is through it." And the truth of that hit me really hard. I didn't like it, but I accepted it. So I do the work I need to do, but I also give myself what I need. Metaphorically speaking, I wear fire-resistant clothing—you know, the kind firefighters wear—heavy boots for walking in treacherous places, and a hat to protect me from unexpected falling objects.

 One of the things that has helped me to heal—and I know this sounds silly—is my pet iguana. Her name is Millie, and she is bright green. I think some bad things were done to me with snakes in the abuse, and Millie kind of looks like a snake. In a way, having her is an attempt to rewrite my past. It is also a way of fighting evil. I can look at her, a reptile all green and scaly, and instead of feeling raw fear, I can see how fundamentally good she is. I can look at her and see the goodness of creation. She is completely innocent—just a beautiful, wild, endearing creature. She reminds me that it was not the snakes, or the children, or the animals that were bad in the abuse; instead, it is that bad things were done *to* these, and this is very different from *being* bad. This sounds so basic and obvious, but it is not always obvious to me or the different parts of me that I split into in order to survive.

Turning Points, Transcendent Experiences

I have had so many transcendent experiences of joy and love, even during the years of the abuse. They are sometimes beyond the power of words to describe. Many of them were what saved me.

Often, transcendent experiences have occurred with spontaneous integration. What I mean is that there have been times when I have just been going along in life, doing my work of healing, and suddenly I become aware inside my head that there is someone there who *wasn't there before*, or whom I wasn't aware of before, and that this person is *talking to me*.

This really is an unbelievable experience—it is as if someone you loved very much died and then came back to life, like in the movie *Ghost*. In fact, I do have one alter who did something like that. She thought she had died because of the stuff they did to her. But one day a couple of years ago, I was lying on the couch, telling myself that I survived, that I was alive, and I heard this voice in my head that said, very quietly and matter-of-factly, "I'm dead." (She had been living in there all these years, having her identity as "the one who got dead.") And so I pulled myself out of my shock—but a *redemptive* kind of shock—and I said, "No, you're not dead." And then, if you can believe it, we had this argument about whether or not she was dead. She didn't want to be alive because she thought the bad people would get her if she were. So she would be very quietly, politely, dead. Except now she was talking to me.

What a compliment that she felt safe enough to talk to me! Wow! I felt like I was in church—but the good kind—or having some mystical experience in nature, because this experience was so undeniably *real*.

There are many things like that in my life, that I can point to or experience, and say, "This is real. This is good. This you did not destroy, and will not, ever, no matter how hard you try. This is God, the transcendent, the holy. This is what matters, and it is with this that I will cast my lot, *not evil*." I know evil, intimately, and I reject it with everything in me. This does not mean that I reject those parts of me that were made to do bad things. I accept them, condemn the ways they were violated, and am thankful for the ways they helped me survive.

And so, I see my life as a kind of ongoing prayer. It goes on all the time, because in every moment, every thought, every action, I feel confronted with that choice between good and evil. It is not merely a theoretical choice. I know I really could go either way. And I continually constitute myself by consciously choosing the good. I know what the alternative is, and I reject it, utterly and absolutely. I want to live my life as a kind of love that is, in the words of a medieval theological concept, "constant creation."

Finding a Good Therapist

I think it is really important for survivors not to settle for just any therapist. Ritual abuse often makes survivors feel like they do not deserve much; sometimes survivors even sabotage themselves by "acting out." But you have been through some awful stuff, and therapy is no time to fool around with some schmuck who does not know what he or she is doing. This would be a waste of your time and money, and a potentially damaging situation for you. You have the right to a competent therapist, and it is your job to find one.

It is good to lay out what you need right from the start. In my recent search for a new therapist, I said in my initial phone calls to hospitals, agencies, offices, etc., that I needed a therapist who had experience dealing with sexual abuse, satanic ritual abuse, and the dissociative disorders or multiple personality disorder. Although it was hard to say this to total strangers over the phone, I think it saved me a lot of time. I also found that the people I spoke with over the phone appreciated my being direct and clear. Finally, I was able to use their responses to this request to gauge their competence in providing what I needed.

In my mind, a therapist treating ritual abuse survivors must, at the very minimum:

1. Believe that ritual abuse exists and have a good understanding of what it entails.
2. Have training and experience in working with other ritual abuse survivors.
3. Have training and experience working with the dissociative disorders (at least one year, ideally more).
4. Be involved in ongoing training and education (such as conferences).
5. Be involved in a supportive network of other therapists doing

the same kind of work (to get support, so he or she can support you).

6. Feel "right" to you, at some gut level. (This is the most important requirement).

I think it is also a good idea to interview at least two or three therapists, both on the phone and in an initial session, to see who feels right to you. In my recent search I did this, and all the therapists I interviewed were very supportive of this. Other good questions to ask prospective therapists are listed in an excellent book called *Secret Survivors*,[1] by E. Sue Blume.

Words of Hope

If I could say a word of hope to a person new in the process, what would it be? I guess I would say several words, but first I would say: "Do what you need to do in terms of self-care to keep from getting too overwhelmed. The hard stuff will be there waiting when you are ready to work on it. But self-care does not happen automatically, and is a skill that must be cultured."

Another thing I would say is that you are not alone. You are not alone in being a survivor of this awful stuff, but you are also not alone in being someone who will heal. Healing really is possible. Look into your past for the ways that you survived. These ways can be healing resources to help you through the pain of the present.

Also, acknowledge your losses. Ritual abuse survivors have experienced loss in ways few others have. These losses are real, and nothing can make up for them. It is okay to remember these losses and to acknowledge those who were lost. I want to say to them, "You were good, and I will love you forever. They tried to make you something terrible, and then to erase you altogether. But I will remember you always, with honor and love." This kind of thing is so painful, but it makes grieving possible. And I believe this is also a way of making those we lost *matter*, or affirming that they always *did* matter, and still do. It is a reaffirmation of love over hate.

I guess the last, and maybe best word of hope I can offer is "love." Love is real, and it matters, and *I love you*. Amen, so be it.

CHAPTER TEN

Long-Term Healing

Under proper conditions, one hundred percent of survivors can heal.
—Laura Davis, *Allies in Healing*

The Healing Journey

When we are in the midst of acknowledging, remembering, and processing the abuse, we feel as though we will never again have a "normal" life. But the healing journey has stages. In the beginning, we are in crisis. There comes a time when we are not in crisis every day; the intensity of healing lessens. There comes a time when we have energy and interest to look outward toward other people, to reclaim parts of ourselves, to develop hobbies and nurture new skills. We will always carry woundedness with us, but those wounds will become less intrusive in our lives.

Long-term healing is a lifelong journey. It is a process rather than an outcome. It is about getting to know oneself, coping with everyday life, healing the wounds on ever-deeper levels, and being open to what new things will come out of that healing. Entering long-term healing means being flexible, ready for new possibilities. It is a process of discovering who we really are, what we like and do not like, learning about the things that support our long-term healing.

Long-term healing has its own pace. We have a lifetime in which to heal. We can choose to work more deeply on issues, and we can take breaks from the hard work of changing our lives. We choose the direction and pace of our healing journey.

This chapter highlights some of the issues that may be faced in the long-term healing journey. It shares the wisdom of those who have gone before and worked through new problems, and it gives ideas about how to meet the challenges.

Building a Balanced Life

When we are in the early years of healing, we have to focus most of our energy on the recovery process. That is okay; it is a necessity. Later we are able to refocus our attention away from our abuse and toward other parts of our lives. We are able to gain a balance between working and playing, struggling and thriving, feeling pain and experiencing joy, being intense and feeling relaxed.

Sometimes it is hard to know how to create a healthy balance. We may have been in pain for so long that we do not know how to let ourselves feel joy. We may have changed so much in the process of healing that we no longer know what we like to do for fun.

Creating a balanced life involves listening to the body to see if we are getting enough sleep or to monitor our stress level. It means listening to the spirit to hear our needs for spiritual nurture. It involves listening to the emotional self to find out whether we need to turn down or turn up the intensity of therapy.

Creating a balanced life requires courage to make the changes that we find. It is hard work to face an addiction or to confront a dysfunctional behavior. It takes courage and persistence to discover oneself and take steps to change. But we are courageous people who have come far in facing the truth and transforming our lives.

Identifying What Is Essential

For me, part of the challenge of creating balance is to identify what is essential to my life and to set priorities accordingly. I have few difficulties in knowing what inner work there is to do. My trouble is in setting limits on that inner work (and my outer work!) and taking breaks in my therapy.

When I was in the emergency stage, I had to stop doing everything except going to work and therapy. It was a big change, because I had been active in many interests. As the times in between crises increased, so did my level of activity. Then I found I was creating crisis by having too many things to do.

It is difficult for me to set priorities. I want to do it all! But I know now that I have physical, emotional, and spiritual limits. I am learning what is essential for me to live in balance, to feel grounded and centered. The essentials are very basic: I need eight hours of sleep per night. I need to read to the kids before I go to bed. I need to exercise regularly and eat healthy food. I need times of self-reflection and spiritual renewal. I need to be with other people in ordinary settings. I need to schedule some fun every weekend. I need to have friends.

When the essentials are in balance, it is easier to set priorities within the rest of my life. It is easier to accept the limitations of time and energy and to live in the moment. I am more grounded, more balanced, more centered.

What are the necessary things in your life? What are the essentials? They may include having a safe place in your living area for the inner children, where they can keep their toys, their crayons and their markers, and where they can display their artistic creations. It may be a requirement that you live near or regularly visit the ocean or the mountains. What are the necessities for your wholeness and balanced life? List them in your journal.

STAYING OPEN TO CHANGE

We have already been through much change—acknowledging abuse, learning about our wounded selves, integrating the realities of our childhood, discovering who we are in recovery. It is difficult to think that we will continue to experience changes, and we may be very resistant to further changes in our lives.

Change can be very threatening to the younger parts of us. Children thrive in safe and secure environments. Change can be scary for children who grew up with many uncertainties.

But change is part of healing . . . and part of life. During long-term healing, we need to be open to opportunities for change—for trying something new, for being willing to adjust to the places that healing may lead us.

Some changes that we will face are minor: different tastes in what we like to eat, what we do for fun, changes in who our friends are, how we spend our time. As we get to know our inner selves better, we may incorporate their likes and dislikes into our day-to-day living.

Other changes are more difficult. We may discover that we need a change of profession or a new job. We may question our sexual orientation. We may face changes in how we relate to our friends or our family of origin. We may be in a relationship that is unable to survive the healing and is ending. Changes may occur in our therapist and helper relationships due to our growth or to life circumstances.

It is normal for us to be in a period of many changes. Until now, we have spent so much time defending ourselves from the abuse and its effects that we may not have developed fully in some areas. Or the abuse may have created a sort of false self which changes and evolves as the true self emerges from healing.

The task in the long-term healing journey is to stay open, flexible, and not too rigid. There is no way to predict who we will become. We are embarking on an exciting trip that will last a whole lifetime. All we have to do is continue to reach for the light, walk toward the wholeness, and open ourselves to the things that support our long-term healing journey.

FACING CHANGE

During times of change, you may feel unbalanced and ungrounded. You may be experiencing fears from a long time ago, and the inner parts of you may be in turmoil. One way to stay grounded is to take some time to remember what your priorities are for today.

Take some time to get centered. Quiet yourself and take some deep breaths. What are you feeling? If you are feeling fear, identify its source. Is it a fear from today? Is there action you can take now in relation to the fear? If necessary, assure the younger parts of you that you are going to keep them safe. Ask them to go to their safe place. When they are settled in, ask yourself the following questions:

1. What are the three most important values in my life today?
2. What are the three most important goals I have for my future?
3. If I am facing change today, is it something that fits with my values and goals?
4. Is it a change over which I have any control?
5. If I can impact the change, what action can I take?
6. If I cannot impact the change, what do I need to do to accept it?

Treatment and Recovery

Over time, we heal. But there may be some parts of our lives that never totally heal. We need not feel shame about having places of weakness. We have already shown great courage and strength in many ways throughout our lives. Part of our long-term treatment is learning how to sort out and cope with these more vulnerable areas of our lives.

ANNIVERSARY REACTIONS

One of the signs that we are healing is improvement in the symptoms of posttraumatic stress disorder. As we heal from the abuse, the flashbacks become less frequent and less intense. Rather than having two, five, or ten flashbacks a week, eventually there will be a time when weeks or months go by between flashbacks. Anxiety, sleep disturbances, and startle response will be reduced. Dissociative episodes may become less frequent.

Some of the effects of trauma, however, stay with us throughout our lives. The woundedness runs deep; and though we heal and the wounds do not hurt as much, there is scar tissue that never goes away. Some folks complain of "an old football injury" that acts up when they try certain physical activities, or "an old war injury" that aches when it rains. We have old war injuries of our own that resurface from time to time.

We may still be ambushed by triggers—sights, smells, sounds, events—that remind us of our abuse. War veterans get triggered by a truck backfiring or a helicopter flying overhead. Survivors may be triggered by a scene in a movie or by the sight of someone who looks like one of our abusers.

There may be certain times of the year during which we are always more sensitive, more vulnerable to the old feelings and memories. It is helpful to be aware that these times of the year bring *anniversary reactions*. In the earlier days of healing, we may have had flashbacks on these days and during these periods. As time goes on, we may not have flashbacks, but we may feel depressed, sad, or angry during these times. It is normal and expected that we will be sensitive to these anniversaries. The abuse was imprinted into our bodies and emotions as well as our memories. Part of healing is learning how to cope with times of vulnerability and how to prepare for the times of year when we may have anniversary reactions.

Anna's Calendar

When I was early in my recovery from ritual abuse, my therapist let me know that most of my flashbacks and difficult periods fell

7 during dates listed on the satanic calendar. I did not want to carry that calendar myself, because I was afraid that I would trigger myself by looking at it. But it was helpful for me to have validation from someone else that what I was experiencing was an anniversary reaction.

Eventually, I adapted the satanic calendar to serve as an anniversary reaction calendar. I listed the dates only, without the names or descriptions of the holidays. My partner put stars on those dates in the yearly calendar. When I am having a hard time with sadness, depression, or dissociation, I can ask if it is a "star day." It usually is. It takes some of the power out of the negative feelings to know that there is a reason I am feeling that way. I can remind myself that it is not happening today, that the feelings being triggered are very old.

I also use the anniversary calendar to help me know when not to schedule important trips, visits to family, etc. I know that particular days such as Halloween or Good Friday are "intensive care" days. I give myself permission to be gentle with myself, to let myself receive nurture and to not expect too much of myself.

If you would like to create or use an anniversary calendar, talk with your therapist. With your therapist's help, create the calendar and decide how you will use it. You do not have to use a satanic calendar to find the dates. You can develop your own calendar by looking back on the times of the year that have been particularly hard for you in the past. Mark these dates on your calendar. If you discover other anniversary reaction times, you can mark those days too.

Plan ahead for the times when you might be more vulnerable. Plan ways to take care of yourself. If you can, try not to schedule things like taking the bar examination, getting married, or delivering a major lecture. Share the schedule with those in your support network. Ask them to call you during that period of time. (If there are several people who make up your support network, you might ask each one to call you on a different day.) Know that it is normal to have periods when you are more sensitive to the wounds of the past and let yourself take the steps to stay safe and comfortable.

THE WOUNDED SELVES

As you move out of crisis and into stability, there will be changes. If you have many inner parts, some of these changes will happen inside of you. You may wonder, or others may ask you, about integration of the parts within you. Integration is one of the many options for healing.

As you recover from the abuse, the wounded parts within you are also healing. Such healing brings change—new likes and dislikes, new interests, new adventures and dreams. The change may be something that you and the ones within you talk about and decide on. Or the changes may happen spontaneously. You may wake up one day to changes within you. Some survivors experience spontaneous integration of two or more of their alters. Some find that the children are growing up. Others choose to create a place within where all can live safely together and add to the creativity and vitality of the whole.

As a caring parent, your role is to help the system work together for the good of everyone. It can be threatening to think about or experience change. As the responsible adult, you may need to assure those inside that nothing will happen to hurt them. You can explain that healing brings growth and change, like when you grow out of your shoes and have to get new ones. You and the inner kids are the ones who have ultimate say in how the system works, whether it changes or stays the same. The solutions are within you and within the system that you created to help you survive.

Meeting Life Challenges

Life stresses for "normal" people present big challenges to ritual abuse survivors. Major events such as divorce, pregnancy, surgery, weddings, and the death of friends or family members can trigger feelings and memories of our abuse. In long-term healing, these events become opportunities for creativity and courage. By this time in our healing, we have skills to deal with the younger parts within us. As we face difficult life situations, we know that we may have to do internal management.

During crises such as divorce, illness, or death, we must draw on the resources of our support network. We do not have to go through these times alone. It is okay to ask for assistance. Talk to your friends and your family of choice. Tell them what is going on with you and what help you need from them. Work with your therapist or other helper to develop a care plan for yourself. Ask for help in thinking ahead about the things that may be especially difficult because of your ritual abuse. Set boundaries for the younger parts within so that the experience does not retraumatize them. Be creative in your problem solving. Remember that life crises are hard for anyone who has to deal with them. Even someone who had a loving, secure childhood will experience struggle and pain in facing the death of a person he or she knows.

WEDDINGS

If wedding ceremonies are a trigger for you, think through a plan before you attend. If your inner wisdom tells you that you should not attend the ceremony, listen to yourself. There are other ways that you can support the couple and join in the celebration. (Write a letter to the couple; send a present; think of or pray for the couple during the time of their wedding ceremony.)

If the wedding is your own, ask your therapist and support people to assist you in thinking through your plan. If you have inner children to care for, you may have a variety of related issues to address with them. (Where are the children during the ceremony? During the honeymoon? If you are moving, where will they live? etc.) Do not forget to plan for your self-care even as you plan for the wedding and reception.

ILLNESS AND DEATH OF FRIENDS OR FAMILY

Death is a hard thing for anyone. Treat yourself gently. There is really no way to prepare for a death. Even when you know it is coming, it is a shock. Know that you may feel bad for a long time. If you have inner children you are caring for, consider asking someone else to take care of them for you.

If you do not know the customs for when someone dies (visitation at the funeral home, a wake, a funeral or memorial service, graveside service, etc.), ask someone to talk through that with you. If you will be participating fully in the activities, ask for the schedule of events—what will happen when. If there is a service, ask to see a copy of what is written, etc.

Once you have the information, make a plan to take care of yourself. If possible, be sure that you have a safe person with you throughout the activities. Tell her or him ahead of time what you may need.

SURGERY

If you must have surgery, listen inside and write down your fears and concerns. Surgery is an intrusive procedure and may be a situation in which ritual abuse survivors face many triggers. ("Normal" people also find it difficult to go through surgery.) Plan ahead as much as you can. If you have inner children, educate them about what will be happening to you.

There are many books that help children to understand about hospitals (see the resources section at the end of this book). Make a plan for where the inner children will be during your surgery and recovery. It is not appropriate for inner kids to go through surgery for you. Be sure that they are in a safe place.

Some survivors have found it helpful to meet the hospital personnel prior to being admitted to the hospital. Ask your doctor to help you meet the anesthesiologist, the recovery room personnel, the nurses who will be working with you during your stay. If you feel comfortable doing so, tell them what your needs might be. Ask your doctor whether you can have a support person with you immediately before your surgery and after your surgery in the recovery room.

You may want to ask your therapist to talk with your surgeon or with the hospital personnel. If you have dissociative identity disorder, inform your psychiatrist about your surgery and ask whether there are any special instructions he or she has for you or for your doctor.

The preparations you do may not be needed, but if you require special assistance during your procedure, you will have set up a supportive community. It is okay to ask for what you need. You are not overreacting. Surgery is a potentially retraumatizing event. Do what you need to in order to care for you and your inner children.

Having Surgery

I was really freaked out about having to have sinus surgery. It was an outpatient procedure. It was considered "minor" surgery, but it was major surgery to me. I was especially afraid of the anesthesia. I knew that the fears were related to my abuse—to being drugged, and lying on tables, and having people doing bad things to me. I had gone through surgery before, and the most frightening time was after surgery when I woke up in the recovery room and felt little and all alone.

I was especially concerned about the time immediately before and after surgery, when I would be under the influence of drugs to make me relaxed and the anesthesia. I was afraid that the younger parts of me would be there, and I would not have an adult present to help them.

I talked to my therapist about this fear. We agreed that I would work hard to have the inner children in a safe place during the surgery. But we also decided that I should plan to have another person with me through the surgery so that if the inner children showed up at the hospital, there would be an adult responsible to take care of them.

My therapist helped me meet the hospital personnel who would be caring for me before and after my surgery. I met the head nurse, the nurse who I would see before the surgery, and the nurse who would be assigned to me in the recovery room. The recovery room nurse explained to me that she would be assigned to two patients at a time and would be sitting between us when I awoke.

On the morning of the surgery, one of my helpers came to stay with me from the time I was admitted until I was under anesthesia. Though she was a nurse, hospital policy did not allow her to be present during the surgery. When I awoke, I saw the recovery room nurse I had met. It was comforting to see a familiar face. At one point I began to call for my mother, and the nurse reminded me where I was and that I was safe.

I'm grateful for all the preparation I did before the surgery. At times I felt silly. But I got through the experience without further harming the little ones inside of me. That made all the preparation really worth it.

Reclaiming the Body

The violation of our bodies in childhood robbed us of many things. We may have lost or never developed a sense of our physical bodies, our sexuality, our ability to feel pain or pleasure. As the flashbacks slow down and we get about the task of thriving, we will inevitably face issues about our bodies. We were often disconnected from our bodies during the abuse. Healing from the abuse gives us the opportunity to experience being in our bodies—to taste food, to see what our body looks like, to feel gentle touch, to learn to live in health and wholeness.

SELF-CARE ASSESSMENT

One of the effects of the abuse is that we did not learn how to care for ourselves, to nurture our bodies, our minds, our spirits. During long-term healing we can turn our energy to looking at some of these issues of self-care.

Ask yourself these questions to help you know how well you are caring for your body:

- *Food and eating:* Do I feel physical hunger when I haven't eaten? Do I feel full when I have eaten enough? Do I know what foods are healthy? what foods are high in fat or sugar? Do I have any symptoms of eating problems (restricting food/self-starvation, bingeing and purging, or compulsive eating)?
- *Self-image:* What is my view of my body? Do I feel accepting of my body? Are there parts of my body that I don't accept, acknowledge, or take care of ? Am I comfortable in my body?
- *Body care:* Do I take care of my body? Do I refrain from smoking, drinking alcohol, or using recreational drugs? Do I regularly have my teeth cleaned and checked by a dentist? Am I able to feel physical pain? Do I have medical checkups regularly? (Persons under age forty-five are recommended to have physical examinations every three to five years. People over forty-five, every two years. For women, annual gynecological exams are recommended.) When I am sick, do I seek medical care?
- *Stress management:* Do I exercise regularly (three to five times a week for twenty minutes)? Do I have symptoms of stress (jaw pains, headaches, neck or shoulder aches, stomach aches or di-

arrhea, greater susceptibility to colds or other illnesses, insomnia)? Do I have times when I am totally relaxed?

Write down the areas of self-care that you need to work on. Which areas seem to be the most important right now? What step will you take first?

If you are unsure of how to get help, ask your therapist or other survivors for their suggestions. There are many books that can help you learn some of the information and skills you will need to improve your self-care. (See "Self-Care" in the Resources section.) Also, there are people who are trained to help you learn about self care. Nutritionists, body workers, touch therapists, and persons who do therapeutic massage can all be your teachers during this part of your healing.

Ask around for professionals who are sensitive to persons who have been abused. Ask other survivors or your therapist for recommendations. If you need to, tell the professional about your special needs as a survivor of ritual abuse. You can also ask your therapist to call and talk to the professional about your needs.

RECLAIMING SEXUALITY

It is common for survivors of sexual abuse to have sexual problems in their adult lives. In ritual abuse survivors, these problems may be compounded. Many ritual abuse survivors experience either sexual addiction or sexual anorexia. Sexual anorexia is a term used to describe a person's aversion to sex. Sexual addiction and sexual anorexia are opposite ends of the spectrum of sexual woundedness. Both are reactions to sexual trauma and barriers to reclaiming one's sexuality.

When we choose to take steps toward developing healthy sexuality, we may uncover one of our most wounded areas. We may discover that we have never had a healthy sexual encounter in our lives, that we are children or adolescents in our emotional-sexual development.

If we are in a relationship with another person, we may have come through a long period of sexual abstinence. Moving back into a sexual relationship may bring up old fears, body memories, or flashbacks. One of the challenges is to locate and nurture the adult within us and to be sure that the child parts are not present during sexual experiences.

Healthy sexuality is made up of much more than actual sexual intimacy. Sexuality includes our awareness of our senses, our relationship with nature, our appreciation and care for our bodies. We cannot have a healthy relationship with other people until we have developed a nurturing and loving relationship with our selves. Ginger Manley writes that there are five dimensions of sexual health:

1. *Personal:* What are my own experiences of sexual victimization and sexual shame?
2. *Relational:* Who am I in relation to someone else?
3. *Behavioral:* What are my sexual behaviors?
4. *Physical:* What is my level of knowledge about the way bodies work?
5. *Spiritual:* How do I connect my spirituality and my sexuality?[1]

You have choice about when and how much to work on reclaiming your sexual self. Treat yourself gently and go at your own pace. There is healing ahead.

Finding Meaning

We have been through a lot—years of abuse, years of pain, years of healing. We have been taken to the bottom of the dark pit of evil, and we have emerged forever changed. We have been stripped of innocence and naiveté; we have seen the fullness of human cruelty. We have invested immeasurable time and money, sweat and tears in learning to live in spite of what we experienced. We have achieved that goal: We are living and breathing, surviving, thriving human beings.

But sometimes, in the midst of it all, we wonder "What is the purpose? What is the meaning in all of this?" We feel trapped in a cycle of endless activity, and we do not know what it is for. We feel that lonely, empty feeling deep inside. We are so caught up in the tasks of surviving and healing that we lose a sense of meaning.

Finding meaning in the struggle is a crucial task during each stage of healing. During the emergency stage, we need at least a tiny spark of meaning to hold on to. It keeps us alive during the times when we wish we had not survived the abuse. When we have moved to the next stage of healing—stabler but still vulnerable—we start to heal the wounds deeper inside of us. We struggle to make sense of all that we have come through. We search for meaning in our spiritual journey, in our relationships with others, in our new awareness of our self and the parts within us.

When we enter into the lifelong process of long-term healing, more than ever we need a sense of groundedness, a sense of meaning in our lives. What does it mean to be moving into the lifestyle of a "normal" person? What does it mean to have friendships with people who are not survivors? What does it mean to terminate therapy or to see our therapist only twice a month? "Who am I now that I am able to function? Who am I now that I do not wake up every day to the memory that I am a survivor?"

This freedom from the struggles of healing can be wonderful. We have more time to do what we like to do, more money to spend on other things, more energy to allocate to living. But the freedom can also feel scary, like there is a void inside. "I don't know who I am without the struggle, without the pain, without wearing the identity of survivor."

Each human being faces similar questions about his or her meaning or purpose in life. Such questions are a part of being human. Whether one is a world leader, a teacher, a factory worker, or a

survivor of something or other, we search for the meaning of our
lives in relation to the lives that surround us, the earth beneath our
feet, the stars in the universe, the presence of a power greater than
ourselves.

When we set apart times to explore what, for us, carries meaning, we are nurturing the spiritual self. We are planting seeds of life
within us.

Helping Others

For two years I lived from crisis to crisis, flashback to flashback.
I could hardly help myself, much less anyone else. I had raging
turmoil inside of me as various inner parts emerged from hiber-
nation and brought with them pieces of the horrible puzzle of
my life.

Often I could not envision any future for myself. I felt that my
life was worthless. I felt that I had been betrayed and robbed of
any meaning or purpose. I was empty and scared.

After a while, I began to receive calls from other survivors. I
was able to give back some of the love and support that others
had given me through the long days and nights. I discovered that
when I shared with others what I had, I received much more in
return. In fact, in order to keep healing, I needed to be able to
reach out to others. That desire to help other people became
one of the anchors that kept me alive. When I was stumbling
from the pain and feeling hopeless, helping others gave my life
meaning.

Exploring Meaning

Finding meaning is a lifelong task. It is also fluid. What is meaningful may change, especially as you grow and develop. Make a
promise to yourself that you will take some time once a year to stop

and see where you are on the inside. Clear your mind of daily details, take some deep breaths, and consider some or all of the questions listed below. Write down your answers in your journal. Over time, they will tell a story of where you have come from, your gifts, your values, your hopes, and your dreams.

1. What are the gifts that I have received from others? (Make a list of everything you can think of.)
2. What are the gifts that I give to others? Are there any special gifts that can come only from me? (Make a list of all the ways you are a gift to other people.)
3. What are the things that I like about myself? my life?
4. What are the things that I would like to change about my life? Are there any steps I can take in the next week?
5. Are there pieces from my journey of healing that have enriched my life? How am I different because of what I have been through?
6. What are the ways that my experience has helped or could help other people?
7. What are the three most important things to me in my life? Which of these three is the most important?
8. What are my dreams about my life? Where do I want to be in two years? five years? ten years?
9. When do I feel most centered, most at peace?
10. Pick one or more of the questions above and draw or paint a picture of your answer.

CHAPTER ELEVEN

For Therapists and Helpers

As therapists we are often charged with the healing of a wounded psyche. . . . But what of the moment when we suddenly realize . . . that we are sitting face to face with a shattered soul?
—Kathy Steele, "Sitting with the Shattered Soul"

Ritual abuse is a world-shattering reality for more than the survivors themselves. There is a very real sense in which even hearing about the abuse can be an experience of victimization. The reality that ritual abuse happens can explode one's world view, one's sense of trust in humanity, one's sense of the power of good in the world.

To accept the opportunity to work with ritual abuse survivors is a courageous step. You will probably have your own inner work to do to be prepared for the realities and horrors that you will inevitably hear about as we survivors share our stories with you. It is crucial for you to do your own work to be able to incorporate this reality into your world view. Your work will follow many of the same steps the survivor will take: believing it is true; feeling anger, grief, fear, and horror over what human beings do to each other; questioning and assessing your beliefs about evil and good, Satan and God; and finding a way of understanding, believing, and claiming spirituality that grounds you deeply in the good.

We as survivors need you to believe what happened to us. Your office may be the only safe place in our world. There may be times when you are the only anchor, stability, and sureness we have left in a life stripped bare by the abuse.

The therapeutic/helping relationship is often critical to our survival. We have an investment in high-quality treatment; sometimes we possess more knowledge than you do about recovering from our abuse. But we want and need your help. We may know a lot about being abused but not very much about living. We need you to be partners with us in the healing process, giving us guidance in remedial living while honoring our creativity, our strength, and our ability to heal.

Suggestions from Survivors

Here are some suggestions for therapists/helpers from survivors of ritual abuse:

1. *Do your own work on your own time.* Learn all you can about ritual abuse, posttraumatic stress disorder, dissociative identity disorder (formerly multiple personality disorder). Get help for your own doubts and troubled feelings. Work on your ability to process your own feelings. Be ready and able to hear difficult stories and feelings. If you are not ready to work with a ritual abuse survivor, refer us to someone who is ready.

2. *Believe that it happened, and tell us you believe us.* Saying, "I believe that ritual abuse is possible" is not enough. Believing means saying, "I believe you. I am sorry that happened to you. It wasn't your fault." Validate our reality. At the same time, do not push *us* to believe before we are ready. We realize that false accusations, while rare, do happen. Help us stay open while our reality is unfolding. But if you have difficulty believing that ritual abuse is real, please refer us to another therapist.

3. *Be sensitive to triggers for ritual abuse survivors.* Don't wear red and black. Be aware that holiday (especially Halloween) decorations may trigger uncomfortable feelings or memories. At your first meeting with a survivor, ask her or him to look around

your office and see if there are any triggers that the survivor is aware of. Be adaptable—move the triggering object, or be willing to arrange for another place in which to work with us. If you are uncomfortable adapting your dress, your environment, etc. to avoid triggers, then be willing and ready to deal with the reactions that we may have.

4. *Be honest with yourself and us.* We survivors of abuse have finely tuned abilities to read other people. (We had to develop these skills in order to survive.) If you are not being honest, we will know. If we discern dishonesty, our reactions will range from confronting you with the truth to sabotaging the relationship because we perceive that you cannot be trusted. Our reaction will depend on where we are in our own recovery.

5. *Be willing to make a long-term commitment to work with us.* Our healing takes a long time and is often very difficult. But we do heal. Our relationship with you may be the first relationship we have ever had that is healthy and trustworthy. It is a relationship that is crucial to our healing. Treat it with respect and care.

6. *If you are learning from us, know that we know that.* Because the treatment of ritual abuse is so new, we may find ourselves in the awkward situation of teaching you how to help us at the same time we are paying for your services. It helps us for you to acknowledge your awareness of this situation, and its unfairness: that we often must teach the ones who care for us; that we have to pay for the healing of wounds we did not deserve, ask for, or have choice in.

Money is a sensitive issue for many of us; it is often a trigger to deep programming. We are often the poorest (financially) of the survivor community. Some of us are unable to work because of our deep wounds. Many of us have committed thousands of dollars to treatment and therapy—just to stay alive. Working with us might mean that we will have to interact regularly with you about difficult money issues.

7. *Be consistent with treatment methods, boundaries, and procedures.* Evaluate critically your own limits around time, telephone contact, etc., and make those limits clear from the start. If you are making changes, talk about them ahead of time, explain the reasons for change, and allow us to ask any questions we might have. If you are going to be out of town, tell us ahead of time and help us know what sort of support we will have when you are gone. Inconsistency or surprises may trigger memories of the abuse and feelings of betrayal.

8. *If you make a mistake, acknowledge it.* If you inadvertently harm us with your error, make amends to us. You have a unique opportunity to model for us healthy relationships. Most of us have never learned how to function in health. We learn how to live with integrity from others around us and from you.

9. *Don't be afraid to share your spiritual beliefs if we ask you spiritual questions.* Don't share your beliefs if we do not bring it up or if you are uncomfortable doing so. There will come a time when we are ready to begin our spiritual healing. You can be an asset to our healing at this time. We may need assurances that you are "on the light side" and have never been and have no intentions of being a person of the dark side. If you feel inadequate answering spiritual questions, encourage us to find someone with whom we can talk about spiritual matters. Some of us have a spiritual director as well as a therapist. Don't be afraid to step into the spiritual realm of therapy if you feel the impulse to do so.

10. *Ground yourself in hope.* We need you to listen to us, to believe us, and to share your hope with us. We need to hear that you have hope for our recovery and hope for our future. We need to hear that you are grounded in hope and that we can also have that groundedness.

11. *If your life is enriched by a therapeutic relationship with us, tell us.* Many of us have never known that we have anything to give anyone. Our relationship with you is a holy, life-giving rela-

tionship. If you receive similar gifts from us, we are further healed by knowing your truth.

Early Stages of Treatment

The early stages of your relationship with us are crucial. There are no shortcuts around the processes of building trust, teaching life skills, and developing networks. We are people who, though deeply wounded, possess tremendous strength, creativity, and capacities to heal. The forces of life that helped us live through our trauma are available now to help us heal from it. We need lots of support and help to get that healing process started. But we need you to understand that your role is helper, coworker, facilitator. The healing comes from within us. You assist in it, but you are not the healing itself. We are greatly helped when you can name and honor our gifts, our strengths, and our ability to heal.

BUILDING TRUST

Trust issues are the first, middle, and last parts of our therapeutic process. We come to therapy so broken by those we trusted that we will continue to struggle with trust for a long time.

To gain our trust, you may need to assure us regularly that you will not hurt us, that you are not "one of them," that you will not go away. You can expect that we will periodically test to see whether you are trustworthy. We might call you in a "safe emergency" to see if you are really there.

You may have to work hard to convince us that you are trustworthy, that you believe us, that you care more about us than our money. You will be challenged to develop your patience. It may be as if we are toddlers first discovering that a parent will come back after he or she goes away. The only way to heal mistrust is for us to experience the process of trusting over time and finding that you are there for us, just like you said you would be.

There are no short cuts to developing trust. Be honest, consistent, and patient. Relate to us with integrity, and you will gain our trust.

TEACHING LIFE SKILLS

Many of us are deficient in basic life skills. We may not have had adequate role models. Or we may have been dissociated over such vast periods of time that we did not learn basic living skills. Part of your job in early stages of therapy may be assessing our level of knowledge and teaching us skills we need for survival.

Our deficiencies may include self-care, relating to others, managing money, and developing healthy boundaries. We may have problems in knowing what to include in a healthy diet. We may not know how make friends or how to handle intimacy. We may have no boundaries. Some of us may not even know such basic things as how to drive, how insurance works, or how to get a telephone hooked up.

We may need encouragement to seek needed medical or dental care. We have been abused by authority figures and may find it difficult to trust persons such as doctors or dentists.

We need help in cognitive restructuring—uncovering the negative or distorted messages we carry and then reprogramming ourselves with positive, reality-based messages.

We also need skills that prepare us for or help us in managing, exploring, accepting, and integrating our trauma. We need to learn parenting skills, management and containment of spontaneous memories/flashbacks, and how to take care of ourselves and our inner parts.

You may not be the one to teach us all these skills. But you are often the one who knows best who we are and how we function. You can assist us in identifying our areas of needed growth and encourage us to find and use the resources around us. Often, all we need is a place to start.

DEVELOPING NETWORKS

One of the greatest gifts for us (and for you) in the early stages of treatment is assisting us in building networks of support. Some of us are active in a recovery or faith community and can find support there. But the nature of our abuse often means that we must build our network of support at a time when it is very difficult to reach out to others. Further, some of us have never developed a support community.

When we enter the early stages of recovery from ritual abuse, we may find that some of the people in our lives are not safe. Other people around us may not be able to handle the nature and intensity of the abuse we experienced. We may become isolated because we are incapable of maintaining old friendships or developing new ones.

We need help in strategizing about who it is safe to tell about our abuse, whether and how to disclose safely, and how to train our network to support us in the ways we need.

This networking may be difficult for us. We were carefully taught not to trust anyone, not to tell about what happened to us. We will be breaking old rules to trust other people, to share with others about our abuse, and to look to others for support. We may need lots of encouragement to reach out and trust others. But it is very important for us to have others in addition to our professional treatment team upon whom we can call.

Encourage us to join a twelve-step group for survivors, help us find a ritual abuse therapy group to join, or assist us in developing contacts with other survivors of abuse. Work with us to identify potential support people in our life. Help us examine our family of origin to determine whether or not they are safe or unsafe for contact.

If our network of support is only you, then it is not large enough. There will come a time when you *and we* will wish we had someone else to call. The broader our network of support, the more secure we are to do our work on ritual abuse.

Caring for Yourself

We need for you to care for yourself. We can be demanding clients and patients, especially during the periods of the year when we experience many anniversary reactions (Halloween, Holy Week, Christmas, solstice and equinox, etc.). If you have more than one client who has been ritually abused, you may be overcome by crises during these times of year.

As much as we want you to be there for us all the time (twenty-four hours a day, 365 days a year), you are human and have limits. We may not want you to have limits, but in the long run, we are better cared for when you are aware of your needs for rest and renewal and are willing to take care of yourself. Also, we learn from you when you acknowledge your limits and practice self-care.

If you do not already have limits on phone calls and contact at home, you may want to consider setting up some guidelines. Rather than fielding all our crises, put your energy into teaching us the skills we need to meet emergencies. Help us have a network of support that is wider than just you. There may still be times when we need your help during evenings, weekends, or holidays. But as we heal, we will be better able to meet challenges ourselves or with the support of our network.

We need consistent rules, boundaries, and limits from you. If you find yourself needing to make changes because of your own circumstances, try to give us plenty of advance warning. Share as much as you can about the reasons for the changes. Be willing to help us process our feelings about the changes.

Work to establish treatment teams for your ritual abuse clients. Such networking will help you to feel connected to others and will help the client know that there is plenty of professional support available. If possible, bring the team together to coordinate a treatment plan. Members of the team may include you, the psychiatrist, the spiritual director, the body worker, the nutritionist, the survivor's spouse or significant other, and members of the person's support network.

Some survivors find that having an ongoing relationship with two therapists is helpful. For example, some survivors have a therapist who works with the child parts and a different therapist who works with adult/current issues. This model allows the client to receive the gifts and strengths from each helper. It also creates a strong back-up system for the times when you are unavailable.

Self-Care Assessment

1. Do I have a comfortable balance between my work and my private life? What is the current percentage of my work life versus my private life?

2. What are the ways that I rest and receive renewal? How often do I take breaks? What additional times of rest and renewal do I need?

3. Do I have adequate boundaries and limits with my clients and patients? What are the procedures I have set up for client emergencies? Do my clients/patients know these procedures?

4. When are the times that are just for me, during which no one else can interrupt?

5. What are my personal limits? Am I aware of when I have reached "compassion fatigue"? What is my plan for such times of personal need?

6. Whom do I call on for professional back-up? Do I have the sense that I am a part of a professional healing network, or do I feel alone in my work?

7. What are my personal beliefs, feelings, and thoughts about ritual abuse? Are there areas of personal, emotional, or spiritual distress that I need to address? Whom can I talk to about them?

8. Do I feel adequately supervised in my work? adequately supported? If not, what can I do to get the supervision and support that I need?

9. Do I feel adequately prepared to assist persons who have been ritually abused? If not, who are others to whom I can refer people?
10. Where do I find grounding? What nourishes my soul? Where do I find hope in times of despair? What can I do to enhance or encourage these parts of my life?

Sitting with the Shattered Soul

This powerful piece is excerpted from an article by Kathy Steele, a therapist who works with adult survivors of severe abuse.[1]

As therapists, we are increasingly confronted with survivors of severe abuse and are being pushed to build new and personal frameworks within which to fit the impact of their experiences. All the therapists I know who do this work have been blindsided at least once by the horror of it. Their own vulnerability, their helplessness in the face of such abuse is staggering. So is the evil. I don't know another word for it. Science has failed us here, so I draw on a spiritual vocabulary. . . .

Sometimes I come home after a difficult session still visualizing a particularly brutal moment in another's life. I cook supper, having an hour before stood again on the edge of a dark chasm. The incongruence strikes me as funny and tragic. It is then that I watch, with awe and relief, the silly antics of my children; their loving bickering; their exquisite vulnerabilities; their ready openness to love and be loved; their earnest, explosive zeal for simply living. They are Life—growing, fresh, clean, good. I am powerfully reminded of all that is this side of my inevitable encounter with death. I have life, I have meaning. I know pain, and I know healing. For now, life is good. I am grateful. I am full. The vast expanse of darkness (my own and that other's) recedes and seems less demanding of my attention than this small and ordinary slice of life in my kitchen. Perhaps I have utilized a dissociative skill to rebalance my security; we see from survivors that one merely exists, but cannot Live, without that security. On the other hand, perhaps this ordinary slice of life contains a greater power than we dreamed: it is a moment pregnant with the possibilities of love and creativity (spontaneity). It is for this that we live.

Then, when we know we will not have all the answers, when we know there are many things bigger than our small selves, we take a deep breath and find a way to put ourselves back into the cradling mercy of goodness. We turn back to the task at hand and find the survivor still sitting on our couch, waiting.

So how do you sit with a shattered soul? Gently, with gracious and deep respect. Patiently, for time stands still for the shattered, and the momentum of healing will be slow at first. With the tender strength that comes from an openness to your own deepest wounding, and to your own deepest healing. Firmly, never wavering in the utmost conviction that evil is powerful, but there is a good that is more powerful still. Stay connected to that Goodness with all your being, however it manifests itself to you. Acquaint yourself with the shadows that lie deep within you. And then, open yourself, all that is you, to the Light. Give freely. Take in abundantly. Find your safety, your refuge, and go there as you need. Hear what you can, and be honest about the rest: Be honest at all cost. Words won't always come; sometimes there are no words in the face of such tragic evil. But in your willingness to be with them, they will hear you; from soul to soul they will hear that for which there are no words.

When you can, in your own time, turn and face that deep chasm within. Let go. Grieve, rage, shed tears, share tears. Find those you trust and let them be with you. Know laughter, the healing power of humor. Trust yourself. Trust the process. Embrace your world, this world that holds you safely now. Grasp the small tender mercies of the moment. Let you be loved. Let you love. The shattered soul will heal.

Courageous Hope

In the fall of 1994 I had an awe-inspiring experience: I helped lead a retreat for a group of families whose children had been ritually abused. Over a period of several years, in a church setting, one hundred children from sixty families had been ritually abused. Twenty survivor children and twenty parents from these families attended the retreat; it was an act of courage. The stories the children told were the stories of my own flashbacks. The pictures they drew looked like the drawings of my inner children.

The event focused on healing from and moving on after the abuse. We led the children in singing, painting, working with clay. We listened to and talked with parents who ached with pain because they had not been able to prevent the abuse. We told stories and played. We talked about safe places and new life and courage and healing.

The children were beautiful, energetic, alive. Some of them looked out at me through deep, wounded eyes; but most of them bore no visible scars.

Our first evening together, I introduced myself: "I am like you. When I was a child, many of the same things happened to me that have happened to you." We met face-to-face, children survivors and adult survivor of ritual abuse.

I couldn't stop looking at these beautiful, brave children. I looked at how alive they were. At how small they were. These children went through the same things I did. I watched their smiles and their energy. I listened to their laughter and their chatter. I felt amazed and honored to be with them. It was a powerful, sacred experience to be sitting among them, talking with them, looking at them.

Whenever I looked up, there were pairs of young eyes looking at me. They seemed amazed to see an adult person who had lived through the same horrors. We stole looks at one another throughout the whole retreat. We were delighted to be in one another's presence—creating, telling stories, and playing.

When I left them, I carried their faces in my mind and in my heart. I still feel a kinship, a bond with those children. I was once their age, their size. Someday they will grow up to be adult survivors, just as I did.

Those children embodied hope and courage for me. And I think, perhaps, I did the same for them. We affirm for one another the powerful, tenacious spirit of life that thrives within each one of us. The abusers could not take that spirit away. We were wounded, broken, and violated. Often we feel pain and face struggles. But now we are healing. Today we *live*—in courage and hope and love.

Definitions

Healing Hearts' Definition of Ritual Abuse[1]

Ritual abuse is any systematic pattern or practice by an individual or a group toward children (or adults who are emotionally and/or physically unable to resist or escape) that constitutes abuse of power in order to harm and control the victim. Such practices may sometimes appeal to some higher authority or power in justification of the actions taken. This abuse may be mental, physical, emotional, spiritual, or sexual.

Ritual abuse is aimed at deepening the silence of the already powerless, the poor, the young, the innocent, the used, and the desperate. Victims are often forced to engage in promiscuous and/or sadistic acts, sacrifices in which one or more persons are tortured and killed, cannibalism, and other provocative and cruel abuses. Society's denial of the existence of ritual abuse must be recognized as an enabling stance that assists in the continued perpetration of these heinous acts.

1. Ritual abuse is torture. It is a calculated effort on the part of perpetrators to systematically brainwash victims through physical, emotional, sexual, and spiritual violation.
2. Perpetrators attempt to destroy basic human values and inculcate their own twisted belief system. Through the use of mental coercion and physical torture they are able to gain control of a victim's thought process and behavior.
3. There is an attempt to distort a victim's sense of self and reality so that he/she feels personally responsible for the heinous acts of violence which are being committed.
4. The child/victim is trained to make and enact violent decisions, and to believe that the desire to behave that way comes out of their own innate evil. Therefore, victims are often unable to hold their perpetrators responsible.

5. Many cult rituals violate state and/or national laws. Abuse can include promiscuous and/or sadistic sexual acts, sacrifices, cannibalism, and other provocative and cruel abuses.

6. Ritualistic crimes are generally motivated by the perpetrators' desire to control and abuse the victims. Any ideology can be used as a justification or a framework for abuse.

7. Often victims are programmed to kill themselves if they ever reveal information about specific rituals and/or the organizational structure and leadership within the cult.

Definitions from the *Diagnostic and Statistical Manual of Mental Disorders Fourth Edition (DSM-IV)*

DIAGNOSTIC CRITERIA FOR POSTTRAUMATIC STRESS DISORDER[2] (DIAGNOSTIC CODE 309.81)

A. The person has been exposed to a traumatic event in which both of the following were present:
   (1) the person experienced, witnessed, or was confronted with an event or events that involved actual or threatened death or serious injury, or a threat to the physical integrity of self or others
   (2) The person's response involved intense fear, helplessness, or horror. Note: In children, this may be expressed instead by disorganized or agitated behavior.

B. The traumatic event is persistently reexperienced in one (or more) of the following ways:
   (1) recurrent and intrusive distressing recollections of the event, including images, thoughts, or perceptions. Note: In young children, repetitive play may occur in which themes or aspects of the trauma are expressed.
   (2) recurrent distressing dreams of the event. Note: In children, there may be frightening dreams without recognizable content.
   (3) acting or feeling as if the traumatic event were recurring (includes a sense of reliving the experience, illusions, hallucinations, and dissociative flashback episodes, including those that occur on

awakening or when intoxicated). Note: In young children, trauma-specific reenactment may occur.

(4) intense psychological distress at exposure to internal or external cues that symbolize or resemble an aspect of the traumatic event

(5) physiological reactivity on exposure to internal or external cues that symbolize or resemble an aspect of the traumatic event

C. Persistent avoidance of stimuli associated with the trauma and numbing of general responsiveness (not present before the trauma), as indicated by three (or more) of the following:

(1) efforts to avoid thoughts, feelings, or conversations associated with the trauma

(2) efforts to avoid activities, places, or people that arouse recollections of the trauma

(3) inability to recall an important aspect of the trauma

(4) markedly diminished interest or participation in significant activities

(5) feeling of detachment or estrangement from others

(6) restricted range of affect (e.g., unable to have loving feelings)

(7) sense of a foreshortened future (e.g., does not expect to have a career, marriage, or children, or a normal life span)

D. Persistent symptoms of increased arousal (not present before the trauma), as indicated by two (or more) of the following:

(1) difficulty falling or staying asleep

(2) irritability or outbursts of anger

(3) difficulty concentrating

(4) hypervigilance

(5) exaggerated startle response

E. Duration of the disturbance (symptoms in Criteria B, C, and D) is more than one month.

F. The disturbance causes clinically significant distress or impairment in social, occupational, or other important areas of functioning.

DEFINITION OF DISSOCIATIVE IDENTITY DISORDER[3] (*FORMERLY* MULTIPLE PERSONALITY DISORDER) (DIAGNOSTIC CODE 300.14)

The essential feature of Dissociative Identity Disorder is the presence of two or more distinct identities or personality states (Criterion A) that recurrently take control of behavior (Criterion B). There is an inability to recall important personal information, the extent of which is too great to be explained by ordinary forgetfulness (Criterion C). The disturbance is not due to the direct physiological effects of a substance or a general medical condition (Criterion D). In children, the symptoms cannot be attributed to imaginary playmates or other fantasy play.

Dissociative Identity Disorder reflects a failure to integrate various aspects of identity, memory, and consciousness. Each personality state may be experienced as if it has a distinct personal history, self-image, and identity, including a separate name. Usually there is a primary identity that carries the individual's given name and is passive, dependent, guilty, and depressed. The alternate identities frequently have different names and characteristics that contrast with the primary identity (e.g., are hostile, controlling, and self-destructive). Particular identities may emerge in specific circumstances and may differ in reported age and gender, vocabulary, general knowledge, or predominant affect. Alternate identities are experienced as taking control in sequence, one at the expense of the other, and may deny knowledge of one another, be critical of one another, or appear to be in open conflict. Occasionally, one or more powerful identities allocate time to the others. Aggressive or hostile identities may at times interrupt activities or place the others in uncomfortable situations.

Individuals with this disorder experience frequent gaps in memory for personal history, both remote and recent. The amnesia is frequently asymmetrical. The more passive identities tend to have constricted memories, whereas the more hostile, controlling, or "protector" identities have more complete memories. An identity that is not in control may nonetheless gain access to consciousness by producing auditory or visual hallucinations (e.g., a voice giving instructions). . . . There may be a loss of memory not only for recurrent periods of time, but also an overall loss of biographical memory for some extended period of childhood. Transitions among identities are often triggered by psychosocial stress.

DEFINITION OF DISSOCIATIVE DISORDER NOT OTHERWISE SPECIFIED[4] (DIAGNOSTIC CODE 300.15)

This category is included for disorders in which the predominant feature is a dissociative symptom (i.e., a disruption in the usually integrated functions of consciousness, memory, identity, or perception of the environment) that does not meet the criteria for any specific Dissociative Disorder. Examples include:

1. Clinical presentations similar to Dissociative Identity Disorder that fail to meet full criteria for this disorder. Examples include presentations in which: (a) there are not two or more distinct personality states, or (b) amnesia for important personal information does not occur.
2. Derealization unaccompanied by depersonalization in adults.
3. States of dissociation that may occur in individuals who have been subjected to periods of prolonged and intense coercive persuasion (e.g., brainwashing, thought reform, or indoctrination while the captive).

Guided Imagery for Creating a Safe Place

Joan Furman

Joan Furman, M.S.N., R.N., is a private practitioner of holistic nursing in Nashville, Tennessee. In her practice, she works with the interaction of mind and body, and offers counseling, healing touch therapies, and other approaches to create a healthful mind/body relationship.

Instructions

Use this guided imagery or visualization to create a safe place. You may create this on your own or ask your therapist or a friend to read it to you. If you tend to dissociate when you do a relaxation exercise, you might want to ask for your therapist's help. Either way, I suggest the following process:

1. Read through the script and decide if it sounds okay to you.
2. Make a recording of the script. (It is much easier to relax if you are listening to your voice or the voice of a safe friend rather than trying to remember what was written.)
3. As you record, remember to *slow down* and lower your natural speaking voice. Leave pauses at the ends of phrases and sentences. Leave longer pauses where you are imagining doing something, such as standing under a waterfall. Talk in as soothing a voice as you have, as though you are calming and soothing a little child. If you want background music in the recording, choose something that is very soothing and won't change beat, tempo, or pitch. Be sure that the music won't stop in the middle of the recording.
4. It will take about twenty minutes to record the imagery. Turn off the phone and be sure that you have a safe and quiet place to record. Remember: speak slowly and pause frequently, at least at the end of each phrase.

5. After you have recorded the imagery, practice the visualization several times, until the pattern becomes clear in your mind and your body responds automatically.

   If, at any time, you feel unsafe, open your eyes, stop the imagery, and reground yourself in today. Get up and do a nurturing activity. Call someone on the telephone and tell them what is happening. You are safe and you have control today.

6. After you have practiced the visualization, you can follow the abbreviated version when you are feeling the need to go into safety. Sit or lie down in your usual position for the visualization. Allow your body and mind to remember what to do. Begin to breathe as you do in your safe place, and take yourself to your safe place.

Imagery for Creating a Safe Place

Allow yourself to be in a comfortable position, either lying down or sitting up. If you're sitting up, place a pillow behind your back, and allow your neck and your back to be nicely supported, not leaning back too much if you have difficulty staying awake. Remember that if you feel afraid at any time, just open your eyes and ground yourself in today. You are safe and you are in control today.

Begin to take a couple of long, deep breaths all the way down into your diaphragm. [Inhale.] Hold it, and as you exhale, let go of the tension. [Exhale.] Letting go. . . . Take another deep breath all the way in. [Inhale.] Allow all the tension to move into your lungs, and then let it go, [Exhale.] just begin to let go. . . . And if you're still feeling tense, repeat that process a few times as you begin to let go, begin to relax. . . . Create a silent and healing space around you. . . . Focus only on your quiet breathing and the sound of my voice. . . . Allow yourself to begin to let go, to create a healing time, a time of peace and safety. . . .

I'm going to count from seven to one. And with each descending number, you'll find yourself becoming more and more relaxed. Relax your body, relax your mind, focus only on your breathing and the sound of my voice and letting go. Seven. . . .

Relax your feet and ankles. Allow your feet and ankles to become very relaxed. Wiggle your toes to let the tension out. . . . Allow this relaxation to drift up into your calves and your knees, relaxing those

muscles in your legs, even relaxing the bones. . . . Allow the relaxation
to drift up into your thighs, relaxing those muscles in your thighs. And
gently relax your hips and your pelvic area. Relax your lower abdomen
all the way to your navel. . . . Relax your lower back. Six. . . .

Let the relaxation gently drift. Let it drift up into your solar plexus
area and into your chest and your lungs, just letting go. . . . Let the relaxation surround your heart and your lungs, and relax. Notice how
gentle and quiet your breathing is becoming. . . . Let the relaxation
drift around to your back. Relax each bone in your back, and all the
muscles and all the nerves, as the relaxation fills your shoulders now,
gently spilling over your shoulders and down to your elbows. . . . Relax
your forearms and your wrists. . . . Relax the palms of your hands and
your fingers. Five. . . .

Relax your neck, all that tension that holds your shoulders up, tight,
around your ears. Let your shoulders drop now, and let the tension go.
. . . Allow the relaxation to drift up the back of your scalp and into your
head. . . . Each breath allows you to become more and more relaxed.
Let the relaxation drift into your eyes, and your nose, and your cheeks.
. . . Your mouth becomes so relaxed, your tongue relaxes enough to
drop away from the roof of your mouth. Your jaw drops just a little. . . .
You're so relaxed. And going deeper, you relax. Four. . . . Three. . . .

More and more relaxed. . . . And two. . . . Scan your body for any
remaining pockets of tension. And let go. . . . And one. . . .

You find yourself in a safe place outdoors. Perhaps it's not a place
you've ever seen before except in the beauty of your own mind. You see a
place outdoors that is beautifully safe. . . . Allow the images to come. . . .
For in this place of safety, only you are allowed. In this place of safety, no
one can come without your invitation. In this place of safety, you are always at peace. . . .

Allow the images to come. . . . Notice the color of the sky at your
favorite time of day. And in this place, at this most perfect time of day,
at the season and the temperature that you like on your skin, allow
your senses to become more and more alive. Look around at the sur-
roundings and allow yourself to see; if not with your eyes, then sense
with your heart. . . . Each time you come to your safe place, you may
develop it and allow it to become more and more beautiful. Allow
yourself to see what is here today. . . . Notice the color of the trees or
flowers or grass, or perhaps sand or water. Let the colors and tex-

tures come alive for you in this beautiful and safe place. . . .

Listen to the sounds of safety. . . . Perhaps you hear birds or splashing or the sound of wind in the trees or the grass. . . . Allow yourself to create a place of safety and peace that is always yours, always safe. . . . And breathe in the safety. And breathe out the fear. And breathe in the safety. And breathe out the fear. . . .

As you breathe in, you can even smell the smells of safety. . . . Perhaps salty air, or the sweet smell of a flower. . . . Breathe in the smells of your safe place. It's so safe here that you can even taste it as you lick your lips. Let yourself bask in the safety and the peace. . . .

Allow yourself to walk around, to be in this place, to notice more and more, to create more and more in this place. . . . Perhaps you would like to build a shelter of some kind, a cottage, a cave, a tent, a tree house. And if it's already there, you may add to it. . . . Plant flowers, adding a splash of color. Add special places or rooms to your safe place. . . . Create anything that you would like. [Long pause.]

Create special places for special kinds of feelings that need to be healed, special places to wash away fear and pain. . . . Create a waterfall or a pool of healing water. Stand under the waterfall to wash away the fear. . . . Let the healing waters wash away what you'd like to be finished with. Each time you come to the waterfall or the healing pool of water, you can wash away more and more of the past. . . . Each time you come, you are cleansed and rejuvenated, the shame is washed away. Wash away the pain. Wash all of it away, as you are ready. [Long pause.] When you are finished, step out of the water and you will find a robe or a towel to dry and warm yourself.

Now allow yourself to continue walking around your safe place. . . . You find a place for a healing garden, a place that is just for your healing. You can plant anything you would like. . . . You can plant wishes and dreams for the future. You can plant seeds of your healing. And you can weed out what you want to be finished with. Take some time to work with your garden now. [Long pause.]

And now, find your favorite place in all of safety. Walk around until you find just the right place. [Long pause.] Sit down, and get comfortable. . . . Breathe in the safety and the peace. Breathe out the fear. . . . Breathe in the safety and peace. Breathe out the fear. . . . Breathe in the safety and peace. Breathe out the fear. . . . And just be in this place as you breathe and heal. . . .

Stay in this place as long as you would like. . . . And when you are ready, simply count yourself out by counting from one to five. When you reach the number five, your eyes will open. And you will be awake and alert, and feeling safe and at peace. One. . . . Two. . . . Three. Take a deep breath. . . . Four. . . . And five.

Short Version of the Guided Imagery

Begin to breathe in the safety and peace. Breathe out the fear. And breathe in the safety and peace. And breathe out the fear. Each time you breathe in, relax your body. And each time you exhale, let go of tension. Breathe in relaxation. Breathe out tension. With each breath, count from five to one. . . . If you need more than that, begin at seven or ten, counting to one. . . . Make each breath a number. Each exhale letting go. As you are counting, as you are breathing, allow the image of safety to fill your mind. . . . You are there, in safety, in peace. No one can be there with you without your permission. Focus only on breathing, on counting, on imagining your safe place once again. Allow your vision to come alive as you breathe. Remember and focus on all the images in your safe place. . . . Breathe in the peace and the safety. Breathe out the fear.

Allow your senses to come alive again in this place. Remember how it looks. Remember all the detail—the color of the sky, the grass or trees or sand or water. . . . Remember your place of safety and how very beautiful it is. . . . As you continue breathing in safety and breathing out fear, remember the sounds of your safe place. . . . Remember how beautiful it smells. . . . Remember the sights—glance around at your house or structure of safe shelter, and see your waterfall or pool of healing water. . . . And over there, see your garden. . . . And remember, remember the beauty and the peace and the safety. . . . Sit as long as you need to, breathing in safety and peace. Breathing out fear, as long as you need to. . . . Do whatever else you need to do in your place of safety. Spend as long as you like. . . . And when you are ready, simply count yourself out by counting from one to five. And as you leave the place of safety, bring with you the knowing that you are safe, you are at peace, and everything is going to be all right.

Notes

Introduction

1. Ellen Bass and Laura Davis, *The Courage to Heal: A Guide for Women Survivors of Child Sexual Abuse* (New York: Harper and Row, 1988).

1. The Basics

1. See John Bradshaw, *Homecoming: Reclaiming and Championing Your Inner Child* (New York: Bantam Books, 1990), or Charles L. Whitfield, *Healing the Child Within* (Deerfield Beach, Fla.: Health Communications, 1988). Other suggestions are listed in the resources section of this book.

2. Bass and Davis, *The Courage to Heal*, 65–69.

2. What Is Ritual Abuse?

1. Healing Hearts, *Ritual Abuse: What Is It?* (Oakland, Calif.: Healing Hearts, 1992).

2. David W. Lloyd, "Ritualistic Victimization," *RoundTable* (spring 1992): 17.

3. Elizabeth Power, *Ritual Abuse: A More Accurate Language and Its Implications* (Nashville, Tenn.: MPD/DD Resource and Education Center, 1993), 2.

4. Ibid., 3.

5. Ibid.

6. *Encyclopaedia Britannica*, 15th ed., s.v. "satanism."

7. Walter C. Young, Roberta G. Sachs, Bennett G. Braun, and Ruth T. Watkins, "Patients Reporting Ritual Abuse in Childhood: A Clinical Syndrome. Report of 37 Cases," *Child Abuse and Neglect* 15 (1991): 182.

8. Bennett G. Braun, "Dissociation: Behavior, Affect, Sensation and Knowledge," in *Dissociative Disorders 1985: Proceedings of the Second Inter-*

national Conference on Multiple Personality/Dissociative States, ed. B. G. Braun (Chicago: Rush University, 1985).

9. *Sexual anorexia* is a term used to describe a person's aversion to sex because of his or her sexual woundedness. Like the eating disorder, anorexia nervosa, it is a part of an overall disease that results from unresolved woundedness. It is no healthier than the opposite end of the spectrum, overeating or addictive sexual behavior.

10. Lenore Terr, *Too Scared to Cry: Psychic Trauma in Childhood* (New York: Basic Books, 1990), 182–83.

11. Ibid., 181. Dr. Terr is a leading researcher in traumatic memory. In this case, she studied the cases of twenty preschool children with documented trauma.

12. Ibid., 163.

13. Ibid.

14. For an interesting discussion of this history, see Judith Lewis Herman, *Trauma and Recovery* (New York: Basic Books, 1992).

15. Sigmund Freud, *The Origins of Psychoanalysis: Letters to Wilhelm Fliess, Drafts and Notes: 1887–1902* (New York: Basic Books, 1954), 215.

16. Roland C. Summit, "The Centrality of Victimization," *Psychiatric Clinics of North America* 12, no. 2 (June 1989): 415.

17. "Holocaust Deniers: Assault on Truth and Memory," *Vanderbilt Today* 33, no. 3 (winter 1995).

18. Deborah Lipstadt, "Holocaust Lecture Series," quoted in "Holocaust Deniers." Lipstadt holds the Dorot Chair of Modern Jewish and Holocaust Studies at Emory University, Atlanta, Georgia. She is the author of *Denying the Holocaust: The Growing Assault on Truth and Memory* (New York: Free Press, 1993).

4. Kid Management

1. Raymond Giles, *Deeply Hurt and Profoundly Confused: Signs and Symptoms of Incest Trauma*, audiocassette (Phoenix: American Audio and Tape Library, 1990).

2. American Psychiatric Association, *Diagnostic and Statistical Manual of Mental Disorders*, 4th ed. (Washington, D.C.: American Psychiatric Association, 1994), 484. (Cited hereafter as *DSM-IV.*)

3. Bennett G. Braun, ed., *Treatment of Multiple Personality Disorder* (Washington, D.C.: American Psychiatric Press, 1986), xiv.

4. Frederick Buechner, *Telling Secrets* (San Francisco: Harper San Francisco, 1991), 98.

5. Sources used include James W. Fowler, *Stages of Faith: The Psychology of Human Development and the Quest for Meaning* (San Francisco: Harper and Row, 1981); Theresa Huntley, *Helping Children Grieve: When Someone They Love Dies* (Minneapolis: Augsburg Fortress, 1991); Sara Covin Juengst, *Sharing Faith with Children: Rethinking the Children's Sermon* (Louisville, Ky.: Westminster John Knox, 1994); Barbara M. Newman and Philip R. Newman, *Development through Life: A Psychosocial Approach*, 5th ed. (Pacific Grove, Calif.: Brooks/Cole, 1991); and Ron Taffel with Melinda Blau, *Parenting by Heart: How to Be in Charge, Stay Connected, and Instill Your Values, When It Feels Like You've Got Only 15 Minutes a Day* (Reading, Mass.: Addison-Wesley, 1991).

5. Reprogramming: Overcoming Mind Control

1. Caryn StarDancer, "Reprogramming Worksheet," *SurvivorShip* 3, no. 8 (August 1991), copyright © 1990 Caryn StarDancer.

6. Loss and Grief

1. Paul Kent Froman, *After You Say Goodbye* (San Francisco: Chronicle Books, 1992), 39.

2. The stages-of-grief model says that people go through different stages (denial, sadness, anger, etc.) more or less in sequence until they have finished their grief work over a particular loss.

3. Froman, *After You Say Goodbye*, 43.

4. Ibid., 40.

5. Elie Wiesel, *The Town beyond the Wall*, trans. Stephen Becker (New York: Avon, 1964), 99.

Interlude III: Living the Questions

1. My current spiritual struggle is reflected in this article by choosing to capitalize only the words *Good* and *Evil*.

2. Harold S. Kushner, *When Bad Things Happen to Good People* (New York: Schocken Books, 1981).

3. Sue Monk Kidd, *When the Heart Waits* (San Francisco: Harper and Row, 1990).

7. Facing Evil

1. Jack Bemporad, "The Concept of Man after Auschwitz," in *Out of the Whirlwind*, ed. Albert H. Friedlander (New York: Union of American Hebrew Congregations, 1968), 483.

2. Kushner, *When Bad Things Happen to Good People*, 81.

3. Aleksandr I. Solzhenitsyn, *The Gulag Archipelago* (New York: Harper and Row, 1974).

4. Joseph Heller, *Catch-22* (New York: Simon and Schuster, 1955), 178.

5. Frederick Buechner, *Telling Secrets*, 31.

6. William Hamilton, quoted in Introduction to *Out of the Whirlwind*, ed. Albert H. Friedlander (New York: Union of American Hebrew Congregations, 1968), 463.

7. Bemporad, "The Concept of Man after Auschwitz," 482–83.

8. Elie Wiesel and Albert H. Friedlander, *The Six Days of Destruction: Meditations toward Hope* (New York: Paulist Press, 1988), 69–70.

9. Jay B. McDaniel, *Of God and Pelicans: A Theology of Reverence for Life* (Louisville, Ky.: Westminster John Knox, 1989), 24.

10. Spalding Gray, in *Swimming to Cambodia*, film (Burbank, Calif.: Warner Home Video, 1987).

11. Elie Wiesel, *The Gates of the Forest*, trans. Frances Frenaye (New York: Holt, Rinehart, and Winston, 1966), 194.

12. Elie Wiesel, *Night*, trans. Stella Rodway (New York: Hill and Wang, 1960), 71.

13. Elie Wiesel, *Twilight*, trans. Marion Wiesel (New York: Summit Books, 1987), 209.

8. Reclaiming Ritual as an Agent of Healing

1. Frederick Buechner, *Wishful Thinking: A Theological ABC* (New York: Harper and Row, 1973), 82.

2. Leonard Bernstein and Stephen Schwartz, "A Simple Song," *Mass* (New York: G. Schirmer, Inc., 1971).

3. "Hush, Hush, Somebody's Callin' Mah Name," in *Songs of Zion* (Nashville: Abingdon, 1981), 100.

4. Gary McLain, *The Indian Way: Learning to Communicate with Mother Earth* (Sante Fe: John Muir Publications,1990).

5. Ibid.

6. Elie Wiesel, *The Gates of the Forest*, 197.

7. Wiesel writes from his experience as a Holocaust survivor. He represents one segment of the Jewish community. Other Jewish persons hold different beliefs and concepts.

9. Healing Our Spiritual Selves

1. Pia Mellody, *Facing Codependence: What It Is, Where It Comes From, How It Sabotages Our Lives* (San Francisco: Harper and Row, 1989), 181.

2. Bernard Bush, S.J., "Reclaiming the Spiritual after Satanic Abuse" (workshop in Worcester, Mass., February 1992, sponsored by Grace Institute, Shrewsbury, Mass.). Father Bush is a Roman Catholic priest who works with ritual abuse survivors.

3. Ibid.

4. Ntozake Shange, *for colored girls who have considered suicide/ when the rainbow is enuf* (New York: Simon and Schuster, 1977), 63.

Interlude VI: Love Is Real

1. E. Sue Blume, *Secret Survivors: Uncovering Incest and Its Aftereffects in Women* (New York: Wiley, 1990).

10. Long-Term Healing

1. Ginger Manley, "Sexual Health Recovery in Sex Addiction: Implications for Sex Therapists," *American Journal of Preventive Psychiatry and Neurology* 3, no. 1 (1991): 33–39. See also Ginger Manley, "Healthy Sexuality: Stage 3 Recovery," *Sexual Addiction and Compulsivity: The Journal of Treatment and Prevention* 2, no. 3 (1995).

11. For Therapists and Helpers

1. Kathy Steele, "Sitting with the Shattered Soul," *Pilgrimage: Journal of Personal Exploration and Psychotherapy* 15, no. 6 (1989): 19, 24–25.

Appendix A: Definitions

1. Healing Hearts, "Ritual Abuse."
2. *DSM-IV*, 427–29.
3. Ibid., 484–85.
4. Ibid., 490.

The Survivor's Glossary of Medical Terms

Add this glossary to your survival kit. These are definitions of some terms survivors may encounter in the course of their treatment.

abreaction. Freud originated this word in his hypnosis work, defining it as a sudden release of emotion, sometimes violent. In today's usage, it often means the reliving of a traumatic experience (with or without the therapist) which releases the feelings associated with that event. These experiences may be spontaneous or planned. (A survivor can plan to work in a safe setting to release the feelings.)

acting out. Destructive behavior. The behavior, "acted out" against oneself or others, may be symbolic of earlier stages in the person's life.

affect. Feeling, emotion.

agitation. Extreme restlessness.

alter. One of the parts, alternative personalities, or inner kids of a person who has multiplicity.

altered state. A condition in which normal patterns of consciousness are qualitatively changed. May be from drug use, meditation, hypnosis, listening to music, triggers, etc.

amnesia. Loss of ability to recall memory. This inability to remember can be caused by trauma. The memory loss can be selective or global.

amnesic barrier. A protective "curtain" that surrounds a memory of trauma and keeps the brain from being aware of the traumatic event.

anger to power. A model of anger work developed and used at Cottonwood Treatment Centers. The anger work follows five steps: (1) Choose a safe way to express yourself (paper tearing, wall pushing, silent scream, towel twisting, empty chair, foot stomping, pillow squeeze, etc.). (2) Say why you are angry. (3) Say what you want, need, prefer. (4) Affirm what is important to you. (5) Make a commitment, goal, for the future.

antidepressant medication. A drug that elevates mood and relieves depression (e.g., Prozac, Zoloft, Pamelor, Norpramine).

antipsychotic medication. A drug used with major psychotic disorders which has a calming effect and reduces delusions and hallucinations (e.g., Mellaril).

anxiety. Low- to high-level fear.

art therapy. Therapy that uses painting, sculpture, and other artistic media as methodology.

atypical dissociative disorder. Dissociative disorder with features of multiple personality disorder.

autohypnosis. Hypnosis that is self-induced.

bataka. Foam bat used to therapeutically express anger.

benzodiazapines. Drugs that reduce anxiety (e.g., Ativan or Xanax).

bipolar disorder. Another name for manic depression.

blocking. Sudden interruption of thought or speech that the person cannot explain. The person is unable to access the previous thought.

body memory. Memories relived in the body's tissues. The survivor feels the physical feelings of the traumatic experience.

borderline personality disorder. A diagnosis used to describe persons who are mistrustful and have mood swings that are not due to bipolar disorder. Survivors may be misdiagnosed as having borderline personality disorder. It is beginning to be recognized that many "borderlines" are abuse survivors.

boundaries. Limitations in physical, emotional, psychic space. Boundaries are often either deficient or excessive in survivors' lives.

brief reactive psychosis. A reaction to major stress that produces problematic psychiatric reactions but does not last longer than a week.

catharsis. An outpouring of emotion, generally regarded as helpful.

cathart. To fart psychologically.

co-conscious. More than one part of the system being conscious at a time.

cognition. Awareness through knowing (perceiving, imaging, reasoning, judging, thinking).

cognitive restructuring. Bringing to light distortions and correcting them.

compartmentalization. The division of feelings, ideas, values within a person.

compulsion. Repetitive actions over which a person has no control.

containment. The skill or ability to hold memories of trauma or to re-schedule work with inner parts until another time.

contracting. Usually refers to making an agreement or promise with someone (perhaps a therapist) in order to create safety or further progress of treatment.

countertransference. A therapist's emotional response to a client.

DDNOS. Dissociative disorder not otherwise specified. (See appendix A for a detailed definition.)

defense mechanism. The process by which one protects the self from undesirable feelings. Also called "ego defenses."

delusion. A false belief that cannot be corrected by reason or irrefutable proof.

denial. A defense mechanism that protects a person from knowing what is true by minimizing its importance. Denial is commonly used to defend against the reality of abuse or the presence of a compulsion.

depersonalization. A symptom of dissociation in which one experiences a loss of personal identity. The body or parts of the body are seen as unreal, large, small, out of proportion, etc.

depression. A state (mood alteration) of despondency, low energy, hopelessness, and difficulty in thinking.

derealization. A symptom of dissociation in which one is unable to perceive things as they really are. An alteration of the perception of reality, the size or shape of objects, etc.

dissociation. Separation of activities and psychological processes from the whole personality. A psychological response to trauma, dissociation protects the child victim by allowing her or him to "leave" the abusive experience.

dissociative disorder (DD). A state in which an individual experiences disruptions of memory, identity, or consciousness. Survivors of trauma frequently develop a dissociative disorder.

dissociative identity disorder (DID). (Formerly called multiple personality disorder.) The fragmentation of the personality into two or more distinct identities or personality states which recurrently take control of behavior. (See appendix A for a more detailed definition.)

DSM-IV. *Diagnostic and Statistical Manual of Mental Disorders,* 4th ed. The diagnostic tool of the American Psychiatric Association.

ego. The self. The executive agency of the personality which controls action and decisions.

ego strength. The psychic energy available to the self, which enables a person to go through difficult experiences.

flashback. The spontaneous reexperiencing of a traumatic event in which the person feels as though the trauma is currently happening.

fragment. A partially developed part of a personality.

fugue. An experience where an individual in a state of amnesia leaves home and changes identities.

gatekeeper personality. A part of the system which has the responsibility to relate to the outside world and protect the inner parts.

grandiosity. Exaggerated image of self or others.

hallucination. Seeing, hearing, smelling, feeling something that is not there. Psychotic hallucination does not refer to what is experienced in a flashback or abreaction.

host. The part, alter, that is in leadership of a person and relates to the world.

hypervigilance. Being on guard; extreme sensitivity to external stimuli; a symptom of posttraumatic stress disorder.

hypnosis. An altered state of consciousness (or trancelike state of mind) induced by a therapist for the purpose of retrieving repressed information. It is characterized by increased suggestibility, relaxation, or alertness.

imprinted injunctions. Programming.

inner child. Concept developed originally for use in recovery from codependency. The "inner child" is the child part of our psyche. "Inner child" or "inner children" are parts of us that—due to trauma, abuse, abandonment, or other childhood issues—need to be cared for and reparented so that the adult may move into a healthy adulthood. Some persons with multiple personality disorder or dissociative disorders prefer to refer to their alters as inner children.

integration. The joining together of alters within a person who has DID so that they work smoothly together in a coordinated whole.

internal helper. A part of the system that works to assist the whole in healthy ways.

intrusive memories. Traumatic recollections or flashbacks that disrupt one's consciousness, sleep, life.

lithium. A drug used to treat manic depression.

major depressive disorder. Extreme and long-lasting depression.

manic depression. A disorder characterized by alternating states of depression and mania (euphoria) in varying states of severity. Characterized by wide mood swings and psychotic behavior.

map. A systematic chart of one's personality.

mapping. A tool for persons with multiplicity by which they can get to know the parts of the system, who they are, how they are structured, and how they are related to each other. Mapping a system can help develop communication, strategy for therapy, and interpersonal support.

memory. The mental function of recalling what has been learned or experienced. This word is used to describe the recall of events which occurred in the past (flashback or abreaction) about which one has been amnesic.

memory warp. Phrase used by survivors to describe the time after a flashback when one has not fully returned to the present. The survivor may be feeling confused, emotional, fuzzy, small, sleepy, etc.

minimization. Downplaying the seriousness of one's pain, one's trauma, one's situation.

MMPI. Minnesota Multiphasic Personality Inventory. A test of 550 questions which measures a subject's similarity to personality variations or disorders.

mono. A person who is not a multiple.

mood. A mild emotion in a transient state.

multiple personality disorder (MPD). (See *dissociative identity disorder [DID]*). The American Psychiatric Association in 1994 changed the diagnosis of MPD to dissociative identity disorder (DID) in the *Diagnostic and Statistical Manual of Mental Disorders*, 4th ed. *(DSM-IV)*.

multiplicity. The preferred term for some survivors with dissociative identity disorder/multiple personality disorder.

Myers-Briggs Personality Indicator. A test that reveals characteristics of one's personality and ways of relating to others and the world.

neuroleptic drugs. Drugs given to help control hallucinations and bizarre thoughts.

neurosis. Any of several less severe personality disorders characterized by rigid and unsuccessful attempts to control anxiety.

neurotic. One who builds castles in the air. (See *psychotic.*)

obsessive compulsive disorder. A diagnosis characterized by ritualistic repetition of unwanted or impulsive thoughts or actions.

out-of-body experience. An experience during which a person feels he or she is located at a point other than where the physical body is, yet still feels to be in a normal state of consciousness. Mystics practice for years to develop this skill; abused children do it instinctively.

panic attack. An instance of overwhelming or paralyzing fear; may include heart palpitations, tremors, nausea, shortness of breath.

paranoia. A state characterized by fear of persecution or delusions of grandeur with no other impairment of intellectual functioning.

persecutor personality. A part of the personality who talks about or acts out self-destructive behavior.

personality disorder. Stable characteristics that cause distress or impair functioning; characterized by daily functioning patterns that inhibit the person's interactions with others and the world.

phobia. Strong, persistent, irrational fear.

posttraumatic stress disorder (PTSD). The development of symptoms such as flashbacks, exaggerated startle response, sleep disorders, etc., following a dramatic, psychologically distressing event. (See appendix A for a more detailed definition.)

programming. Messages that are imprinted into the unconscious as a part of the abuse.

protector personality. A part of the personality whose job is to protect the system or parts of the system.

psychodrama. Experiential group therapy in which therapists guide a participant to recreate an event or environment from his or her past in order to bring forward the feelings associated with it and thereby resolve or heal the event or environment.

psychopharmacology. The study of drugs used to affect the mind and behavior.

psychosis. A mental disorder characterized by behavior indicating loss of contact with reality.

psychosomatic. Describes a physical ailment of psychological origin.

psychotic. A psychotic lives in castles built in the air. (See *neurotic.)*

rapid switching. Moving quickly from one part or alter to another.

rationalization. Justifying an irrational act or thought by interpreting it in terms of some motive other than the one that is actually responsible.

recovery. One's journey of healing and health.

reenactment. The conscious or unconscious recreation of one's trauma or aspects of one's trauma.

regression. The act of returning to an earlier stage of one's life or development. Regression is also used therapeutically to describe an intentional return to an experience of trauma in order to bring to consciousness what has been unconscious. (See *abreaction.)*

reparenting. The process of self-care in order to assist in the healing of wounded child parts.

repetition compulsion. The impulse to reenact an earlier experience regardless of whether it is helpful or not.

repression. An unconscious process of keeping experiences out of the conscious mind.

resistance. An instinctive opposition to attempts to uncover the unconscious. (Or, a word that therapists use to mean that the client is not doing what they want her or him to do.)

revictimization. Repeated subjection to violence or trauma.

revolving door phenomenon. When groups of patients are hospitalized, discharged, and readmitted in a frequently recurring pattern.

safe place. An imaginary location where parts of one's personality, one's inner kids, may reside with safety and security.

schizophrenia. A chronic mental disease which manifests itself in severe disturbances of thought processes, emotions, and the perception of reality. It may be caused by biological rather than environmental factors. Sometimes survivors of trauma are misdiagnosed as having schizophrenia.

selective amnesia. Remembering some things and not others.

self-hypnosis. Autohypnosis. The ability to hypnotize oneself. Persons with dissociative disorders are frequently able to achieve self-hypnosis.

self-mutilation. Physically injuring the self.

self-stimulating behavior. Repeated stimulation of oneself ranging from actions such as rocking to destructive actions such as hitting one's head.

shame. A feeling of self-hatred.

sleep disorders. A symptom of posttraumatic stress disorder: having trouble falling asleep, staying asleep, or waking early; insomnia; nightmares; night terrors.

somatization. Body memories; physical reexperiencing of trauma.

splitting. A process of dissociation; creation of a new entity. Also used to refer to borderlines playing one person against another, or seeing people as all good or all bad.

startle response. An emotional and physical response to unexpected stimulation. When exaggerated, it is often a symptom of posttraumatic stress disorder.

sublimation. Modifying an instinctual activity or motive so that one more acceptable to society is substituted. A healthy ego does this naturally.

suicidal ideation. Thinking about or having fantasies about suicide.

suppression. The conscious putting away into the unconscious mind of an idea or experience that would cause anxiety if it were left in awareness.

survivor. A person subjected to abuse; preferred over "victim."

survivor guilt. Feelings resulting from being one of few survivors of a disaster or violent experience.

switching. Going from one alter to another.

system. The organization of personalities or fragments of personalities within a self.

therapeutic alliance. Having a good working relationship with a therapist.

transference. Projecting thoughts, feelings, ideas onto the therapist or other person. Responding to the therapist as though he or she were some significant person in the patient's past.

trauma. An injury; something that is either physically or psychologically hurtful.

trauma pocket. Area of consciousness in which memories of abuse are stored; it often can be accessed through personalities connected with specific trauma.

trigger. An event or circumstance that reminds a survivor of abuse; it can bring on a flashback or spontaneous memory.

waking self. Part of a system most often present, performing daily functions such as going to work, buying groceries, etc.

Resources

Ritual Abuse

Cooper-White, Pamela. "Ritualistic Abuse." In *The Cry of Tamar: Violence against Women and the Church's Response*. Minneapolis: Fortress Press, 1995.

Hudson, Pamela S. *Ritual Child Abuse: Discovery, Diagnosis and Treatment*. Saratoga, Calif.: R & E Publishers, 1991.

Los Angeles County Commission for Women. *Ritual Abuse: Definitions, Glossary, the Use of Mind Control*. Los Angeles: LACCW, 1989. (Available for $5.00 from L.A. County Commission for Women, 383 Hall of Administration, 500 Temple St., Los Angeles, CA 90012.)

Oksana, Chrystine. *Safe Passage to Healing: A Guide for Survivors of Ritual Abuse*. New York: HarperPerennial, 1994.

Roney-Wilson, Kathleen. "Healing Survivors of Satanic Sexual Abuse." *The Journal of Christian Healing* 12, no. 1 (spring 1990): 9–12.

Rose, Elizabeth S. "Surviving the Unbelievable: A First-Person Account of Cult Ritual Abuse." *Ms.* (January/February 1993): 40–45.

Ryder, Daniel. *Breaking the Circle of Satanic Ritual Abuse: Identifying and Treating the Hidden Trauma*. Edited by Jane T. Noland. Minneapolis: CompCare, 1992.

Sakheim, David K., and Susan E. Devine. *Out of Darkness: Exploring Satanism and Ritual Abuse*. New York: Lexington Books, 1992.

Satanic Ritual Abuse: The Current State of Knowledge. Special issue of *Journal of Psychology and Theology* 20, no. 3 (fall 1992). A journal for professionals. This special issue presents professional dialogue about satanic ritual abuse and MPD, its veracity and its treatment. Of special note is an article by Martha L. Rogers, "A Call for Discernment—Natural and Spiritual."

Smith, Margaret. *Ritual Abuse: What It Is, Why It Happens, and How to Help*. San Francisco: HarperSanFrancisco, 1993.

StarDancer, Caryn. *Returning to Herself.* Book of poetry and art. Available for $9.00 (includes postage) from Caryn StarDancer, P.O. Box 1284, Lakeport, CA 95453.

StarDancer, L. J. *Turtleboy and Jet the Wonderpup: A Therapeutic Comic for Survivors of Ritual Abuse.* Kelseyville, Calif.: H.P.L. Publishing, 1989. Available for $7.00 (includes postage) from Caryn StarDancer, P.O. Box 1284, Lakeport, CA 95453.

Stimson, Eva. "Evil among Us." *Presbyterian Survey* (September 1993): 13–18. The story of a local church that discovers satanic activity in its midst.

SurvivorShip: A Forum on Survival of Ritual Abuse, Torture, and Mind Control. Bimonthly publication written by survivors and professionals. Send self-addressed stamped envelope with inquiry to SurvivorShip, 3181 Mission St. #139, San Francisco, CA 94110.

Dissociative Identity Disorder (Formerly Multiple Personality Disorder)

Adams, Ann. *The Silver Boat: The Discoveries of Separateness, Adventures of Oneness.* Cincinnati: Behavioral Science Center, Inc., Publications, 1990. An illustrated parable/story about a journey of multiplicity.

Braun, Bennett G. *The Treatment of Multiple Personality Disorder.* Washington, D.C.: American Psychiatric Press, 1986.

Cohen, Barry, Esther Giller, and Lynn W., eds. *Multiple Personality Disorder from the Inside Out.* Dallas: Sidran Press, 1991.

Gil, Eliana. *United We Stand: A Book for People with Multiple Personalities.* Walnut Creek, Calif.: Launch Press, 1990.

Many Voices: A National Bi-monthly Self-Help Publication for Persons with Multiple Personalities or a Dissociative Process. Newsletter available for $30.00 a year ($36.00 outside the United States) from Many Voices, P.O. Box 2639, Cincinnati, OH 45201-2639.

Pia, Jacklyn M. *Multiple Personality Gift: A Workbook for You and Your Inside Family.* San Jose, Calif.: R & E Publications, 1991.

Power, Elizabeth. *Managing Our Selves: Building a Community of Caring.* Nashville: E. Power and Associates, 1992. A workbook on self-management for persons with multiple personalities or dissociative disorders. $17.95 plus $4.00 (shipping and handling). Available from

E. Power & Associates Products, P.O. Box 2346, Brentwood, TN 37024-2346.

Putnam, Frank. *Diagnosis and Treatment of Multiple Personality Disorder.* New York: Guilford Press, 1989. A classic in the study of MPD.

Roberts, Susan C. "Multiple Realities: How MPD Is Shaking Up Our Notions of the Self, the Body, and Even the Origins of Evil." *Common Boundary* (May/June 1992): 24–31.

Rosik, Christopher H. "On Introducing Multiple Personality Disorder to the Local Church." *Journal of Psychology and Christianity* 11, no. 3 (fall 1992): 263–68.

Healing from Abuse

Bass, Ellen, and Laura Davis. *The Courage to Heal: A Guide for Women Survivors,* rev. ed. New York: HarperCollins, 1994.

Blume, E. Sue. *Secret Survivors: Uncovering Incest and Its Aftereffects in Women.* New York: Ballantine, 1990.

Bradshaw, John. *Healing the Shame That Binds You.* Deerfield Beach, Fla.: Health Communications, 1988.

―――. *Homecoming: Reclaiming and Championing Your Inner Child.* New York: Bantam, 1990.

Davis, Laura. *Allies in Healing: When the Person You Love Was Sexually Abused as a Child—A Support Book for Partners.* New York: HarperCollins, 1991.

Feldmeth, Joanne Ross, and Midge Wallace Finley. *We Weep for Ourselves and Our Children: A Christian Guide for Survivors of Childhood Sexual Abuse.* San Francisco: HarperSanFrancisco, 1990.

Froman, Paul Kent. *After You Say Goodbye.* San Francisco: Chronicle Books, 1992. This book presents a model for dealing with the grief of multiple losses.

Hickman, Martha Whitmore. *Healing after Loss: Daily Meditations for Working through Grief.* New York: Avon Books, 1994.

Hopkins, Khristine. *Survivors: Experiences of Childhood Sexual Abuse.* Berkeley, Calif.: Celestial Arts, 1994.

Lew, Mike. *Victims No Longer: Men Recovering from Incest and Other Child Sexual Abuse.* New York: Harper and Row, 1988.

Maltz, Wendy. *The Sexual Healing Journey: A Guide for Survivors of Sexual Abuse*. New York: HarperPerennial, 1992.

Manley, Ginger. "Healthy Sexuality: Stage 3 Recovery." In *Sexual Addiction and Compulsivity: The Journal of Treatment and Prevention* 2, no. 3 (1995).

Mellody, Pia. *Facing Codependence: What It Is, Where It Comes from, How It Sabotages Our Lives*. New York: Harper and Row, 1989.

Whitfield, Charles L. *Healing the Child Within*. Deerfield Beach, Fla.: Health Communications, 1988.

Self-Care

Borysenko, Joan. *Minding the Body, Mending the Mind*. New York: Bantam Books, 1987.

Boston Women's Health Book Collective. *The New Our Bodies, Ourselves: A Book by and for Women*. New York: Simon and Schuster, 1992.

David, Marc. *Nourishing Wisdom: A Mind-Body Approach to Nutrition and Well-Being*. New York: Bell Tower, 1991.

Fowler, George, and Jeff Lehr. *Teaching Your Heart to Dance Cookbook: Natural Recipes and Reflections for Peace and Joy*. Memphis, Tenn.: The Wimmer Companies, 1993.

Ivker, Robert S. *Sinus Survival: A Self-Help Guide for Allergies, Bronchitis, Colds, and Sinusitis*. New York: Putnam Publishing Group, 1992. This book is about sick sinuses, but it covers many self-care issues, including boosting the immune system and a discussion of holistic specialties.

Joy, Brugh W. *Joy's Way: A Map for the Transformational Journey*. New York: G. P. Putnam's Sons, 1979.

Krieger, Dolores. *The Therapeutic Touch: How to Use Your Hands to Help or to Heal*. Englewood Cliffs, N.J.: Prentice-Hall, Inc., 1979.

————. *Accepting Your Power to Heal: The Personal Practice of Therapeutic Touch*. Santa Fe: Bear and Co., 1993.

Rosenthal, Norman E. *Winter Blues: Seasonal Affective Disorder—What It Is and How to Overcome It*. New York: Guilford Press, 1993.

Parenting

Coles, Robert. *The Spiritual Life of Children*. Boston: Houghton Mifflin, 1990.

———. *Their Eyes Meeting the World: The Drawings and Paintings of Children*. Boston: Houghton Mifflin, 1992.

Darian, Shea. *Seven Times the Sun: Guiding Your Child through the Rhythms of the Day*. San Diego: LuraMedia, 1994.

Fowler, James W. *Stages of Faith: The Psychology of Human Development and the Quest for Meaning*. San Francisco: Harper and Row, 1981.

Groseclose, Kel. *Why Did God Make Bugs and Other Icky Things?* Nashville, Tenn.: Dimensions for Living, 1992.

Huntley, Theresa. *Helping Children Grieve: When Someone They Love Dies*. Minneapolis: Augsburg Fortress, 1991.

Hynson, Diana L., ed. *To the Point: Confronting Youth Issues: Violence*. Nashville, Tenn.: Abingdon Press, 1994. Chapter on "Ritual Abuse" makes suggestions for adults who work with youth.

Juengst, Sara Covin. *Sharing Faith with Children: Rethinking the Children's Sermon*. Louisville, Ky.: Westminster John Knox, 1994. See chapters on "How Children Grow in Faith" and "The Spiritual Needs of Children."

Leight, Lynn. *Raising Sexually Healthy Children*. New York: Rawson Associates, 1988.

Stein, Sara Bonnett. *A Hospital Story: An Open Family Book for Parents and Children Together*. New York: Walker and Co., 1974.

Taffel, Ron, with Melinda Blau. *Parenting by Heart: How to Be in Charge, Stay Connected, and Instill Your Values, When It Feels Like You've Got Only 15 Minutes a Day*. Reading, Mass.: Addison-Wesley, 1991.

For Children

Aliki. *Feelings*. New York: Mulberry Books, 1984.

Baylor, Byrd. *I'm in Charge of Celebrations*. New York: Charles Scribner's Sons, 1986.

Bruchac, Joseph, and Jonathan London. *Thirteen Moons on Turtle's Back: A Native American Year of Moons*. New York: Philomel Books, 1992.

Cohen, Caron Lee. *The Mud Pony: A Traditional Skidi Pawnee Tale*. New York: Scholastic, 1988. A poor boy becomes a powerful leader when Mother Earth turns his mud pony into a real one. But after the pony turns back to mud, he must find his own strength.

Garbarino, James. *Let's Talk about Living in a World of Violence: An Activity Book for School-Aged Children*. Chicago: Erikson Institute, 1993.

Martin, Bill, Jr., and John Archambault. *Knots on a Counting Rope*. New York: Henry Holt, 1987.

McLain, Gary. *The Indian Way: Learning to Communicate with Mother Earth*. Santa Fe: John Muir Publications, 1990.

Ramshaw, Gail. *Sunday Morning*. Chicago: Liturgy Training Publications, 1993. A beautifully illustrated book that introduces a child to the parts of the Christian worship service.

Rogers, Fred. *Going to the Hospital*. New York: Putnam's Sons, 1988.

Wood, Douglas. *Old Turtle*. Duluth, Minn.: Pfeifer-Hamilton Publishers, 1992.

Spiritual Recovery

Cummings, Louise. *Eyes Wide Open: Spiritual Resources for Healing from Childhood Sexual Assault*. Winfield, B.C., Can.: Wood Lake Books, 1994.

Flaherty, Sandra M. *Woman, Why Do You Weep? Spirituality for Survivors of Childhood Sexual Abuse*. New York: Paulist Press, 1992.

Foote, Catherine J. *Survivor Prayers: Talking with God about Childhood Sexual Abuse*. Louisville, Ky.: Westminster John Knox, 1994.

Leehan, James. *Defiant Hope: Spirituality for Survivors of Family Abuse*. Louisville, Ky.: Westminster John Knox, 1993.

Norberg, Tilda, and Robert D. Webber. *Stretch Out Your Hand: Exploring Healing Prayer*. New York: United Church Press, 1990.

Wuellner, Flora Slosson. *Prayer and Our Bodies*. Nashville, Tenn.: The Upper Room, 1987.

――――. *Heart of Healing, Heart of Light: Encountering God Who Shares and Heals Our Pain*. Nashville, Tenn.: The Upper Room, 1992.

Theological Reflection

Blumenthal, David R. *Facing the Abusing God: A Theology of Protest.*
  Louisville, Ky.: Westminster John Knox, 1993.
Horton, Anne L., and Judith A. Williamson, eds. *Abuse and Religion:
  When Praying Isn't Enough.* New York: Lexington Books, 1988.
Kushner, Harold S. *When Bad Things Happen to Good People.* New York:
  Avon Books, 1983.
McDaniel, Jay B. *Of God and Pelicans: A Theology of Reverence for Life.*
  Louisville, Ky.: Westminster John Knox, 1989.
Poling, James Newton. *The Abuse of Power: A Theological Problem.*
  Nashville, Tenn.: Abingdon, 1991.
Wiesel, Elie. *The Trial of God (As It Was Held on February 25, 1649, in
  Shamgorod): A Play in Three Acts.* Translated by Marion Wiesel. New
  York: Random House, 1979.

Traumatic Memory and Backlash

The Coalition for Accuracy About Abuse, 1310 Clinic Dr., Tyler, TX
  75701. A network of nonaffiliated individuals and organizations
  committed to promoting accuracy and advocacy about abuse.
Freyd, Jennifer J. "Personal Perspectives on the Delayed Memory
  Debate." *Treating Abuse Today* 3, no. 5 (1993): 13–20. A public
  response by the daughter of the founders of the False Memory
  Syndrome Society.
Herman, Judith Lewis. *Trauma and Recovery.* New York: Basic Books,
  1992.
Herman, Judith Lewis, and Mary R. Harvey. "The False Memory
  Debate: Social Science or Social Backlash?" *Harvard Mental Health
  Letter* (April 1993): 4–6. Available for $4.00 from Harvard Mental
  Health Letter, Dept. BI, 1164 Longwood Ave., Boston, MA 02115-
  6092.
Lipstadt, Deborah E. *Denying the Holocaust: The Growing Assault on
  Truth and Memory.* New York: Free Press, 1993.
Summitt, Roland C. "The Centrality of Victimization." *Psychiatric
  Clinics of North America* 2, no. 2 (June 1989): 413–30.
Terr, Lenore. *Too Scared to Cry: Psychic Trauma in Childhood.* New York:
  Basic Books, 1990.

————. *Unchained Memories: True Stories of Traumatic Memories, Lost and Found.* New York: Basic Books, 1994.

For Helpers

Hover-Kramer, Dorothea, Janet Mentgen, and Sharon Scandrett-Hibdon. *Healing Touch: A Resource for Health Care Professionals.* Albany, N.Y.: Delmar Publishers, 1996.

Nouwen, Henri. *The Wounded Healer.* Garden City, N.Y.: Doubleday, 1972.

Steele, Kathy. "Sitting with the Shattered Soul." *Pilgrimage: Journal of Personal Exploration and Psychotherapy* 15, no. 6 (1989): 19–25.

Organizations

These organizations provide services related to ritual abuse. Send SASE with inquiries.

Believe the Children, P.O. Box 26-8462, Chicago, IL 60626. Phone: (708) 515-5432. Promotes awareness about sexual and ritual abuse.

Cult Awareness Network, 2421 W. Pratt Blvd., Suite 1173, Chicago, IL 60645. Phone: (312) 267-7777. Education about cult activity.

Monarch Resources, P.O. Box 1293, Torrance, CA 90505-0293. Phone: (310) 373-1958. Information clearinghouse.

Multiple Creations, 1238 1st Street, Brandon, Manitoba R7A 2Y6 Canada. Phone: (204) 725-2741. Publishes newsletter for MPD/DD survivors. Referrals, resource library, education.

SurvivorShip, 3181 Mission #139, San Francisco, CA 94110. Phone: (707) 279-1209. Provides information on ritual abuse survivor issues. Education and professional consultations. Publishes bimonthly newsletter for survivors.

Bibliography

American Psychiatric Association. *Diagnostic and Statistical Manual of Mental Disorders*. 4th ed. Washington, D.C.: American Psychiatric Association, 1994.

Bass, Ellen, and Laura Davis. *The Courage to Heal: A Guide for Women Survivors of Child Sexual Abuse*. New York: Harper and Row, 1988.

Bemporad, Jack. "The Concept of Man after Auschwitz." In *Out of the Whirlwind*, edited by Albert H. Friedlander. New York: Union of American Hebrew Congregations, 1968.

Bernstein, Leonard, and Stephen Schwartz. "A Simple Song." *Mass*. G. Schirmer, Inc., 1971.

Blume, E. Sue. *Secret Survivors: Uncovering Incest and Its Aftereffects in Women*. New York: John Wiley and Sons, 1990.

Bradshaw, John. *Homecoming: Reclaiming and Championing Your Inner Child*. New York: Bantam Books, 1990.

Braun, Bennett G. "Dissociation: Behavior, Affect, Sensation, and Knowledge." In *Dissociative Disorders 1985: Proceedings of the Second International Conference on Multiple Personality/Dissociative States*, edited by B. G. Braun. Chicago: Rush University, 1985.

———, ed. *Treatment of Multiple Personality Disorder*. Washington, D.C.: American Psychiatric Press, 1986.

Buechner, Frederick. *Telling Secrets*. San Francisco: HarperSanFrancisco, 1991.

———. *Wishful Thinking: A Theological ABC*. New York: Harper and Row, 1973.

Bush, Bernard, S.J. "Reclaiming the Spiritual after Satanic Abuse." Workshop in Worcester, Mass., February 1992, sponsored by Grace Institute, Shrewsbury, Mass.

Darian, Shea. *Seven Times the Sun: Guiding Your Child through the Rhythms of the Day*. San Diego: LuraMedia, 1994.

Fowler, James W. *Stages of Faith: The Psychology of Human Development and the Quest for Meaning*. San Francisco: Harper and Row, 1981.

Freud, Sigmund. *The Origins of Psychoanalysis: Letters to Wilhelm Fliess, Drafts and Notes: 1887–1902*. New York: Basic Books, 1954.

Friedlander, Albert H., ed. *Out of the Whirlwind*. New York: Union of American Hebrew Congregations, 1968.

Froman, Paul Kent. *After You Say Goodbye*. San Francisco: Chronicle Books, 1992.

Giles, Raymond. *Deeply Hurt and Profoundly Confused: Signs and Symptoms of Incest Trauma*. Audiocassette. Phoenix: American Audio and Tape Library, 1990.

Healing Hearts. "Ritual Abuse: What Is It?" Oakland: Healing Hearts, 1992.

Heller, Joseph. *Catch-22*. New York: Simon and Schuster, 1955.

Herman, Judith Lewis. *Trauma and Recovery*. New York: Basic Books, 1992.

"Holocaust Deniers: Assault on Truth and Memory." *Vanderbilt Today* 33, no. 3 (winter 1995).

Huntley, Theresa. *Helping Children Grieve: When Someone They Love Dies*. Minneapolis: Augsburg Fortress, 1991.

Juengst, Sara Covin. *Sharing Faith with Children: Rethinking the Children's Sermon*. Louisville, Ky.: Westminster John Knox, 1994.

Kidd, Sue Monk. *When the Heart Waits*. San Francisco: Harper and Row, 1990.

Kushner, Harold S. *When Bad Things Happen to Good People*. New York: Schocken Books, 1981.

Lipstadt, Deborah E. *Denying the Holocaust: The Growing Assault on Truth and Memory*. New York: Free Press, 1993.

Lloyd, David W. "Ritualistic Victimization." *RoundTable* (spring 1992): 17.

Manley, Ginger. "Healthy Sexuality: Stage 3 Recovery." *Sexual Addiction and Compulsivity: The Journal of Treatment and Prevention* 2, no. 3 (1995).

———. "Sexual Health Recovery in Sex Addiction: Implications for Sex Therapists." *American Journal of Preventive Psychiatry and Neurology* 3, no. 1 (1991): 33–39.

McDaniel, Jay B. *Of God and Pelicans: A Theology of Reverence for Life*. Louisville, Ky.: Westminster John Knox, 1989.

McLain, Gary. *The Indian Way: Learning to Communicate with Mother Earth.* Sante Fe: John Muir Publications, 1990.

Mellody, Pia. *Facing Codependence: What It Is, Where It Comes from, How It Sabotages Our Lives.* San Francisco: Harper and Row, 1989.

Newman, Barbara M., and Philip R. Newman. *Development through Life: A Psychosocial Approach.* 5th ed. Pacific Grove, Calif.: Brooks/Cole, 1991.

Patterson, David. *In Dialogue and Dilemma with Elie Wiesel.* Wakefield, N.H.: Longwood Academic, 1991.

Power, Elizabeth. "Ritual Abuse: A More Accurate Language and Its Implications." Nashville: MPD/DD Resource and Education Center, 1993.

Richardson, Beth A. "Davida Angelica Roared." *Alive Now* 21, no. 3 (1991): 44–46.

Richardson, Jan L. *Shared Journeys: A Woman's Book of Daily Prayer.* Nashville: Upper Room, 1995.

Shange, Ntozake. *for colored girls who have considered suicide / when the rainbow is enuf.* New York: Simon and Schuster, 1977.

Solzhenitsyn, Aleksandr I. *The Gulag Archipelago.* New York: Harper and Row, 1974.

StarDancer, Caryn. "Reprogramming Worksheet." *SurvivorShip* 3, no. 8 (August 1991).

Steele, Kathy. "Sitting with the Shattered Soul." *Pilgrimage: Journal of Personal Exploration and Psychotherapy* 15, no. 6 (1989): 19–25.

Summit, Roland C. "The Centrality of Victimization: Regaining the Focal Point of Recovery for Survivors of Child Sexual Abuse." *Psychiatric Clinics of North America* 12, no. 2 (June 1989): 413–30.

Swimming to Cambodia. Burbank, Calif.: Warner Home Video, 1987.

Taffel, Ron, with Melinda Blau. *Parenting by Heart: How to Be in Charge, Stay Connected, and Instill Your Values, When It Feels Like You've Got Only 15 Minutes a Day.* Reading, Mass.: Addison-Wesley, 1991.

Terr, Lenore. *Too Scared to Cry: Psychic Trauma in Childhood.* New York: Basic Books, 1990.

Whitfield, Charles L. *Healing the Child Within.* Deerfield Beach, Fla.: Health Communications, 1988.

Wiesel, Elie. *The Gates of the Forest.* Translated by Frances Frenaye. New York: Holt, Rinehart, and Winston, Inc., 1966.

————. *Night.* Translated by Stella Rodway. New York: Hill and Wang, 1960.

————. *The Town beyond the Wall.* Translated by Stephen Becker. New York: Avon, 1964.

————. *Twilight.* Translated by Marion Wiesel. New York: Summit Books, 1987.

Wiesel, Elie, and Albert H. Friedlander. *The Six Days of Destruction: Meditations toward Hope.* New York: Paulist Press, 1988.

Young, Walter C., Roberta G. Sachs, Bennett G. Braun, and Ruth T. Watkins. "Patients Reporting Ritual Abuse in Childhood: A Clinical Syndrome—Report of 37 Cases." *Child Abuse and Neglect* 15 (1991): 181–89.

Index

abuse, being forced to harm others, 76, 98–99, 115–16, 121–23, 141, 201

abusers: amnesia in, 27; attitude toward, 141–42; contact with, 14; profile of, 26–27

age-level development, 59; chart, 62–63; sexual, 182–83; spiritual, 149–51

alternate identity (alter), definition, 204. *See also* inner child

amnesic barrier: in the abuser, 27; as defense mechanism, 4; description of, 8; response to trauma, 47, 203–4

anniversary reactions: coping with, 173–76; crisis for therapists and helpers, 194

balance: healthy, 170–71; for therapists and helpers, 195–96

BASK model, 21–22

behavioral memory, signs and symptoms of abuse, 21–24

belief that abuse occurs, 28; society, 16–17, 24–26; therapists and helpers, 166, 187–88; yourself, 22–24

body: care of, 170–71, 180–82; memories, 21; reclaiming, 180–83

boundaries: description of, 34–35; developing, 35–36; with family, 14–15, 93–94; for inner child, 60,

66–68, 70, 177; limits for self, 6, 171; for therapist and helper, 190, 194–95

calendar, 22, 174–76

celebration: of life events, 124–25; of seasons, 132–34

centeredness. *See* grounding

change, 171–73; in therapy, 172, 190, 194

Christian ritual: in healing process, 43; triggers, 144, 159

churches: and abuse, 144; nurturing spirituality, 158–60; and triggers, 159

co-consciousness, description, 49–50

communication, with inner selves, 54

coping skills, to survive abuse, 4, 8, 46–50

courage, 1–2, 198–99

creativity. *See* imagination

crisis: anniversary reactions, 173–76; coping with, 6, 8–14; lessening of, 169

death: age-level understanding, 62–63, 149; coping with, 177–78

denial: of abuse, 22–23; as defense mechanism, 4; of the Holocaust, 25–26; of ritual abuse, 24–26, 201

despair, coping with, 11–14

Printed in the United States
53247LVS00002B/86